# Money $marts
## *for*
# Turbulent Times

# Also by Judith Briles

Stabotage! How to Deal with the Pit Bulls, Snakes, Skunks, Scorpions & Slugs
    in the Health Care Workplace
Zapping Conflict in the Health Care Workplace
The Confidence Factor—Cosmic Gooses Lay Golden Eggs
Money Smarts—Personal Financial Success in 30 Days!
Stop Stabbing Yourself in the Back
Woman to Woman 2000
The Briles Report on Women in Healthcare
10 Smart Money Moves for Women
Smart Money Moves for Kids
Divorce—The Financial Guide for Women
GenderTraps
The Confidence Factor—How Self Esteem Can Change Your Life
When God Says NO
Money Sense
The Money $ense Guidebook
Raising Money-Wise Kids
Woman to Woman
Judith Briles' Money Book
Faith & $avvy Too!
Money Phases
The Woman's Guide to Financial Savvy
The Workplace
Self-Confidence and Peak Performance

**Co-Authored Books**
The SeXX Factor
The Dollars and Sense of Divorce
The Workplace

---

Articles and information of Judith's books
are available on her website, www.Briles.com

# Money $marts

## *for*

# Turbulent Times

*Master
Your
Personal
Finances
in 30 Days!*

# Dr. Judith Briles

**mile high press**

This book is intended as a general guide to the topics discussed. It is not intended and should not be used as a substitute for professional advice (legal or otherwise). You should consult a competent financial planner, attorney or other professionals with specific issues, problems or questions you may have.

Although every precaution has been taken to verify the accuracy of the information contained herein, the author and publisher assume no responsibility for any errors or omissions. No liability is assumed for damages that may result from the use of information contained within.

Company names, and trademarks used in the book belong to the companies that own them. There is no attempt to appropriate these names and trademarks and none should be construed. Also, there is no endorsement, implied, or otherwise, of the companies listed in this book. They are used to illustrate the types of places, software or information centers where readers can find more information. The company names, phone numbers, addresses and websites may have changed since the publication of this book. Finally, **Money $marts**, **Money Smarts** and **Money $marts for Turbulent Times** are used interchangeably within the text. If you wish to contact Judith Briles, her website is *Briles.com*.

Books may be purchased in quantity and/or special sales by contacting the publisher, Mile High Press, Ltd. at PO Box 460880, Aurora, CO 80046; 303-885-4460, faxing 303-627-9184 or email at MileHighPress@aol.com.

Published by Mile High Press, Ltd., Aurora, Colorado.   *MileHighPress.com*
Design by WESType Publishing Services, Inc., Boulder, Colorado

Library of Congress Cataloging  2009920129

Briles, Judith, 1946-
    Money $marts for Turbulent Times: Personal Financial Success in 30 Days!

ISBN: 978-1-88533-131-1

10  9  8  7  6  5  4  3  2  1

1. Finance, Personal.    2. Parenting.

First Edition      Printed in Canada

*For Kathryn and Barb*

# Contents

# Money and You

*Every woman, man and family needs a
Purse/wallet of their own!*

*Welcome to the instant money society*—just about anything you want is available and at your fingertips. If you want it, you can get it. It's only a phone call, the Internet, a short car ride and a charge card away. It's so easy . . . and that's the problem. Too quick, too indulgent, too easy!

Money. Can you live without it? For that matter, can you live with it? Money is one of the many tools that you will use to get what you want and need. If you are like most, you really don't have a full picture of how your money is spent or where it goes. All you know is that money seems to run out before the end of the month does.

The good news is—you are not alone. The bad news is—you have plenty of company.

**Money $marts** is your new partner. It will change the way you think, prioritize and act about money. It will not promise you an instant fix; an instant fix is part of the problem. Rebuilding and redirecting ingrained attitudes and habits about money takes more than one 30-day span.

But, I will promise you this: As you work through the next 30 days, you will see how to eliminate many of the toughest obstacles. It doesn't matter if you are a family of one or one of multi-generations under the same roof. There are basic steps. Some, so simple that you will tell yourself, "I know this stuff." Others, a little more complicated, but definitely doable.

I won't tell you to do weird things with your money or suggest strategies that only someone with a very fat checkbook could accomplish. The tips and tools you will read each day are designed for anyone who is willing to do my recommended "To Do" items. Some days, just a phone call to an organization with a short letter follow-up will be that day's activity. On others, more time is needed.

## How to Use This Book

In **Money $marts for Turbulent Times: Personal Financial Success in 30 Days!,** you will find that it is designed to be read on a daily basis: one reading per day for the next 30 days. Each daily reading will provide you with a brief introduction to a specific topic (***To Think About***) and work space for you to respond either in writing or action (***To Do***). At the end, you will receive one final recommendation (***Money $marts Tip***).

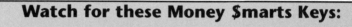

**Watch for these Money $marts Keys:**

**To Think About**

**To Do**

**Money $marts Tip**

**The Money $marts thing to do is to clear your calendar for the next 30 days.**

This chapter and the next are intended to be read as "warm-ups" and not counted in the 30-day total. We'll be looking for attitudes and fears about money.

Acquiring **Money $marts** takes commitment and time. Some days will have a few hours of work; others, a quick read. Some days include strategies for working with kids. If you have none or yours have grown and gone, then you pick up a few days "off."

No matter what, it's an intense month ahead. You will spend over 10,000 days making money. Surely, 30 days in figuring out what to do and how to do it is a drop in the bucket of life—and a critical drop it is.

Your 30-Day project is divided into the following areas:

- Face Your Money Fears (Read before you start the month—this will be a primer to cross over the money resistant barriers.)
- Assessing Your Situation-Getting Started    (Days 1-7)
- Developing Your Plan                         (Days 8-11)
- Setting Up Your Safety Net                   (Days 12-17)
- Family Talks                                 (Days 18-20)
- Kids, Money and College                      (Days 21-23)
- Investing Savvy                              (Days 24-27)
- Building Your Resources                      (Days 28-30)
- Month 2-Review

As you work through the daily readings and activities, realize that the day-by-day strategies, suggestions and actions are presented in a general format. Some of them may not be relevant to you and your family, others you may want, and need, more in-depth. *Building Your Resources* (Days 28-30) is designed for just that purpose. Since some of the days will take more time than others, it may be better to schedule them when you have a day off or a weekend.

In the end, some will be fun and some a quasi-pain-in-the-neck—usually because you are forced to look in the mirror and acknowledge that your money habits have gotten a tad out of hand. **Money $marts** will become your guidebook through the money maze, a maze that is full of detours, potholes and barriers.

Many of the activities will take time to complete. *The use, and misuse, of money will impact you and your family for the rest of your lives.* What's a few hours, even days, when you are implementing **Money $marts** for the rest of your life?

## The Money Fiasco of 2008

No one could have come through 2008 without feeling some form of financial squeeze. For some, it was an unbelievable financial disaster that caught so many off guard.

People I knew lost their jobs, their homes, their life savings-here yesterday, gone today. Poof . . . it felt like it was an overnight happening.

Fat 401(k) accounts were slashed to a fraction of what they were just months earlier; homes that many counted on to yield a hefty part of their retirement seed plummeted in value; and the credit markets turned venomous. The perfect storm. Financial scandals, scams and corruption fermented everywhere.

In the late fall of 2008, I was speaking in Grand Rapids, North Dakota. One of the participants approached me afterward and told me that she had bought the original version of **Money $marts** in 2004 and immediately implemented its game plan. Now, this version, **Money $marts for Turbulent Times** is not "heavy" or "deep" . . . it's not complicated. It's old-fashioned, basic . . . and that's what my reader was telling me. She was financially fine, thank you . . . she felt that her copy of **Money $marts** had saved her financial life.

***Money $marts Tip:*** The bottom line? Simply this: get started. Today. Stay focused. Learn from whatever mistakes you make. Reevaluate what you are doing on an annual basis. Don't let anyone (including yourself) get you derailed. Finally, celebrate your new commitment to financial independence.

With the redirection of your moneys, present and future, any "Will I have to eat cat food?" fears are not forecast for you. Are all the *Money $mart Moves* I shared with you doable? You bet. Just do it!

# Face Your Money Fears

*You aren't born with a fear or attitude about money,
but guaranteed, you've got a few.*

**To Think About:** Fears and attitudes—be they good, bad or ugly—have been developed over a period of time. No doubt, your upbringing is a major contributing factor. Past experiences—successes and failures—create an umbrella or flooring. Then there's the current culture norm—always ready to jump in and give its two bits worth via the media, your circle of friends, even the government.

Let's face it. You are the steward of your money—however big or small your pocketbook or stash, you are in charge of its destiny . . . at least during its initial leg of the money journey.

## The Fear of Being Poor

The number one fear that has been shared during the past year in my *Money $marts* workshop is the fear of being poor—will I have to eat cat food when I stop working?

Years ago, a client had asked me if I would take the time to go visit his mother. He told me that she had some investments, lived mostly off the dividends, interest and her monthly Social Security. He asked that I just check in with her to see if she was getting a decent return on her portfolio. From his brief synopsis of her situation, nothing seemed unusual.

I made the appointment and spent a pleasant two hours getting to know Martha. She was in her early sixties at the time and healthy. She believed that she was a good steward of her money. With financial data filled out, I promised to get back to her within the week with an update on several stocks and suggestions for any changes to her portfolio. As I got up to leave, Martha said, "What about my stash?"

"Stash," I responded, "what stash?"

She pointed to the corner of her living room. All I saw was a big green, over-stuffed chair. "My stash . . . in the chair. . . and drapes." This was a first for me. A whole new stash, rainy day, liquidity fund (more on that later) vehicle!

My new client had stashed in excess of $30,000 over the years in her over-stuffed green chair with matching draperies. She had lived through the Depression—never again would she, or her family, be without food if bad times hit again. It took me over a year to convince her to move her moneys to a money market fund that would earn her interest.

Did she move the entire amount? Nope—at least not initially. Her bottom line number was that she insisted on a stash of $5,000 in the house, money that she could tap into for a movie, food, play, repairs, anything. The good news is that she did move the rest to interest bearing accounts. She signed on for check writing privileges and after two years, finally accepted the fact that she really could access her moneys by writing a check and depositing it into her regular checking account.

The reality is that whether you are rich, poor, or in-between, the person that you are going to have to rely the most on to keep *you* from the poorhouse is you . . . your creativity, your imagination, your intuition, your smarts.

## The Fear of Losing Money

At some point, everyone loses money. It can be from a bad investment, misplacing moneys, inflation erosion, failure to act or make a decision on your investments, fear of making the wrong decision, or fear of losing a job or other resource of funds.

In many cases, men make more money in the workplace than women do (if money is lost in a bad investment, a common male attitude is that it can simply be replaced). Women are less likely to take the financial positions and risks that men often do. A lot of it has to do with familiarity. Men, as boys, still get the majority of money messages from their families, friends and peers.

Working with, and investing money does not have to start in giant steps. In fact, it's wise to avoid them. Start with small steps. Whether it's putting money in a mutual fund (many will allow you to start with as little as $100, if you commit to putting in a minimal amount on a monthly basis), a money fund, or a fund for the kids (or yourself), small amounts can build into fortunes.

Starting small allows you to learn along the way. A little here, a little there. If some of the "little" doesn't work out—the investment fails, or never grows in value (also a failure), you and your net worth won't be destroyed.

## The Fear of Talking About Money

Your upbringing will most likely be the primary factor that shapes your money practices. Most adults "wish" that they had had training and guidance about money and investing as they grew up.

If you came from one of those families that actively discussed money and its many facets, good for you. But, you need to realize that you are in the minority. Not all of your friends will be on the same wave length as you are in money matters. Your awareness, and possibly non-intimidation to the topic, may actually intimidate them!

## The Fear of Making Mistakes and Failing

Everyone makes mistakes. I wished I had $10 for each one I've made over the past 50 years plus. There's no question that if you do make a mistake with your money you aren't going to be happy about it.

---

Mistakes happen. You get to choose—will they handicap and paralyze you? Or will you look at them as a learning and growth experience?

---

What you have to guard against is the reaction that the fear of failure and making mistakes can generate paralysis . . . getting stuck mentally. Making money mistakes and experiencing failures won't destroy you. Your key to resurrecting yourself is determining—

- What happened?
- What factors could you control, influence or alter?
- What factors could you not control?
- What did you learn, the pros and cons?

### The Fear of Creating and Sticking to a Plan

How many incredibly lucky people do you know who win money—lots of it? I bet very few, if any. None of my friends, acquaintances, colleagues or the 30,000 plus people I speak to on an annual basis have ever told me that they have won big money.

In fact, no one has ever told me that they have won more than a few hundred dollars playing blackjack or the slots in Las Vegas.

> Creating a plan means making a commitment. *To yourself.* And, that's where the fear factor enters. If it is in writing, it means that you are supposed to do it versus just talk about doing it. And granted, that can be scary.

Once "it" is in writing, it is easier to track, measure and evaluate the author's progress—yours. Financial plans are guide tools that start you on a path that will lead you to your stated money goals, if followed. They are not, though, set in granite. Times and circumstances change. So do investments and investment opportunities. That means that you don't create it and then stick it in the drawer. It means the plan needs to be reviewed, at least once a year. Financial plans should be *flexible.* Life changes. You change.

You can create a financial plan in one of two ways—do it yourself, or hire a professional. I opt for the professional, preferably a Certified Financial Planner™ Professional. If you do it yourself, you may do fine, but you could easily stumble along the path; if you hire a planner, a road map will be created that is designed for you. The next step is that it's up to you to put your foot on the gas and get going. The commitment part.

## The Fear of Borrowing Money

Ideally, you would like to pay cash for everything. "Ideally" and what's "practical" are not always on the same track. Sometimes, it makes sense to borrow money. Unless you have a big savings account, borrowing money to buy a home is a necessity for most. But, over-borrowing and too much credit is quite common. Borrowing too much should be feared. It's easy to get out of control.

Weekly, your mail box probably has offers of new credit cards—the deal of the week! Should you sign on?—it depends. Ask—

- Do you need the credit card? (It makes sense to have at least one.)
- If you carry a balance, is the interest rate lower than the one(s) you presently have?
- If you don't carry a balance, what's the incentive for you to switch?

If you are contemplating borrowing money for a large item, or already have—a home or an education loan—increase your pay back amount by 10%. Why? Simply this—you will reduce the time your loan payoff paid by approximately one-third. That means you save big dollars and limit the time you "owe" someone. In the case of a credit card, use it by only charging the amount you will pay back within the grace period in the month when you get your bill. That way, no interest will be charged.

In determining whether you should borrow or not, ask yourself if you *need* the item or do you *want* it. If you want it and can't (or aren't sure) you can pay off the amount over the designated time, don't purchase it. If you "need" the item, and can pay it off over the determined payoff time, purchase it. In reality, most people get in trouble when they let their "wants" dictate how money is used.

## The Fear of Investing

Anyone who was half-awake as the new Millennium drew near in 2000 knew that the stock market was hot—it seemed as though everyone and anybody was making money. So, which way should you go? Stocks, bonds, mutual funds, real estate, business opportunities—the list of possibilities is long.

One of the scary things about investing is that there are no guarantees. Any money that you invest can increase in value, maintain its original value, or decline in value.

Sometimes, too many options can confuse you. Should you throw in the towel and give up? Absolutely not. Over time, which means you start investing now, investments, especially the stock market, have outperformed other investments. One of the

*Momisms* of life is "Be patient, your turn will come." Investing takes time and patience. When it comes to investing, don't focus on what your investment is worth this week or even this month. Concentrate on the long haul—what are the projects you are saving for five, ten years from now?

## The Fear of Not Trusting Yourself and Keeping the Wrong Advisors

For women, it is not uncommon to be more loyal to money advisors—bankers, lawyers, accountants, Realtors, insurance agents, stock brokers and financial planners—than to their own money. It's also common to defer to others any action and recommendations of what to do with their money.

Two key differences exist between men and women when it comes to money advisors.

- Women tend to form a type of friendship with their advisors, not wanting to terminate the relationship even if there are signs of poor advice or management.
- Women are more inclined to abdicate financial decisions to someone else. They rarely follow up on what is suggested or done to their financial accounts. This is a direct result of upbringing influences.

In the 15 years I advised women and men about their money, my goal was to get them involved and to not advocate giving their investment and money strategy decisions to me or to any other advisor. It takes time to work through the maze of options. Advisors can help . . . but, so can you.

Think of all the times you have said, "I *knew* it was the right thing to do," or "I knew it was going to happen . . ." Trust yourself. Get involved.

## So, What Are Your Fears?

Everyone has at least one. It's time to confront your deepest financial fears and get them out in the open. Is it becoming a bag lady, dining on cat food or having to rely on others to put food on the table and shelter over your head? The fear of making a mistake that is financially catastrophic can inhibit you from action. Start identifying your fears. Write them down. Just the mere fact that they are on paper opens the door for you to commit and confront them head-on.

*To Do:* As you process through the money maze with this book, you will learn new things—about yourself and others, and how you, and they, relate to money. Learning new things enables you to look at your backpack of fears and do some assessing.

- Are my fears realistic in today's environment?
- Are they relevant to what I currently do?
- Do they hinder me from moving on?
- Are they life threatening (to my spouse, partner, kids or job, my friends, me)?

By identifying your fears, you are doing something quite positive. It's a big plus for you to acknowledge and eventually confront the fears of your upbringing and societal influences—producing a new you. By writing down your fears, you can create their opposites. *Write yours down now.*

Put them in "reminder" letters or notes you write to yourself. Get some Post-it® notes, use them and put these sticky reminders in places where you normally look throughout the day—the mirror in your bathroom, the refrigerator door, your desk or work area, on the telephone handle. By writing down the old, and creating the new, you birth a new script for your life.

**My money fears are:**

_____

_____

_____

_____

_____

### *To Do:* **Ways to Remove Money Fears from Your Life**

The suggestions below are meant to be done over a period of a few months—not all today; you'd never complete them!

## 1.   Enroll in a mini or short class taught at your local community college by a financial professional.

Be aware that most of these classes are presented by individuals as part of their marketing efforts—they hope to get you as a new client. Your initial goal in attending the class is to learn—the jargon, strategies and what your investment options are. You are never under any obligation to become a client.

## 2.   Start an investment club with some of your friends.

It's a great way to learn about stocks with a minimal dollar commitment (starting at $25 a month) and have fun. Contact the NAIC (National Association of Investors Corporation) at 877-275-6242 for an information packet or go online at *better-investing.org*. As a member, you will receive their magazine, *Better Investing*.

## 3.   Find out where your money goes.

Did you spend any money where you now feel you made a mistake in doing so or determined that you really could have waited? Did you feel stupid . . . or did you learn something—as in, "I won't waste money this way again." You'll be doing this exercise within the first week of the **Money $marts** program. Ideally, this is something you should monitor for a full three months—keep track of where every dime lands. Don't forget the frozen yogurt, magazines and the three dollars you misplaced.

**4. If you have kids over 6, plan a monthly money powwow and talk about what items your family "needs" versus "wants" and how much they cost.**
Your objective is to create (and uncover) topics, issues or concerns about money that can be talked about. Make sure the discussion level is when that connects and is understood by the ages present.

**5. Host a potluck dinner at your house with your friends.**
Tell them that it will be a "can you top this" tale about the goofiest or stupidest thing that they have done with money. The objective is to show that no matter how bad it looked or seemed at the time, each survived.

**6. Trust your instincts.**
Do a little mental probing—when was there a time(s) that you didn't follow your own beliefs or "gut feelings" and you were right in the first place? Once you commit to learning about and

using money more effectively, you'll find that "your" feelings and gut reactions are often right on target.

## 7.   Find out what your money is really earning.

Call your bank and ask your representative or someone in customer service how much money would you have in 20 years if you put $100 in a savings account that earned 3% per month every month during that period of time. Many of the banks that offer online services have financial calculators available on their websites—if they do, use them.

Now, call a brokerage company, such as Charles Schwab & Co (800-724-7526 or go online at *schwab.com*) and ask the same thing, but *change* the percent you will receive to what the average growth rate of a growth mutual fund in a top 20% ranking has been the past five years as the percent of growth you will receive for the next 20 years. Go to the Internet, *morningstar.com* and identify a fund from the ones identified under growth. Which yields more—the 3% bank account or the non-guaranteed mutual fund?

## 8.   Think—have you ever put money into an investment and had it decline in value?

Why did it decline—was the stock market down in general; was the industry you're investing in experiencing negative publicity;

was the company losing money or reporting poor earnings? Did the loss cost you anything besides money (loss of sleep, mistrust of the person who recommended you invest the money, negative feeling about investing in general, etc.)?

9. **Remember a time that you were afraid to do an activity (any activity will do) because you didn't understand how to do it or how it worked . . . and you did it anyway, and it worked out well?**
What did you learn—that you were just lucky . . . or that sometimes you don't need to know everything there is to know to move ahead?

***Money Smarts Tip:*** There will always be some type of fear. Cartoon character Pogo said it best, "I have seen the enemy and the enemy is us." By bringing up your awareness level, identifying which fears influence your money decisions, you will achieve the first level of smart money.

# Money $marts . . . 30-Day Overview

| | | | |
|---|---|---|---|
| Pre-30 Day<br><br>Intro to Your<br>30-Day Plan | Pre- 30 Day<br><br>Face Your<br>Money Fears | Day **1**<br><br>Having and<br>Using Money | Day **2**<br><br>Getting<br>Organized |
| Day **6**<br><br>Income<br>Sources | Day **7**<br><br>Uncle Sam and<br>You | Day **8**<br><br>Your Money<br>$marts Goals | Day **9**<br><br>Spending Plans<br>that Work |
| Day **13**<br><br>Other<br>Insurance | Day **14**<br><br>When There's a<br>Will, There's a<br>Way | Day **15**<br><br>Planning a<br>Comfortable<br>Retirement | Day **16**<br><br>Savings that<br>Work |
| Day **20**<br><br>Keeping<br>Holidays in<br>Perspective | Day **21**<br><br>Financing<br>College Without<br>Going Broke | Day **22**<br><br>Savings,<br>Spending,<br>Sharing and<br>Allowances | Day **23**<br><br>The Teen<br>Challenge |
| Day **27**<br><br>Investing in<br>Yourself | Day **28**<br><br>Don't Fall for a<br>Bad Deal | Day **29**<br><br>Hiring the<br>Experts | Day **30**<br><br>Your Money<br>$marts Resource<br>Center |

| Day **3** | Day **4** | Day **5** |
|---|---|---|
| Credit . . . Friend or Foe? | Your Net Worth | Where Does Your Money Go? |
| Day **10** | Day **11** | Day **12** |
| To Bank . . . or Not to Bank | Borrowing for Today . . . and Tomorrow | Insure . . . Maybe! |
| Day **17** | Day **18** | Day **19** |
| Giving . . . What Goes Around, Comes Around | Credit Revisited | Dark Clouds Can Surface |
| Day **24** | Day **25** | Day **26** |
| Your Shelter: Buying vs. Renting | Investing ABCs | To Market, to Market |
| Month **2** | Post **30**-Day | |
| Adding It All Up! | Afterword | |

# Part I
## Assessing the Situation
## —Getting Started

## (Days 1 – 7)

# 1 Having and Using Money

*The problem for most is not that they don't have money;
it's what they do with the money they have.*

**To Think About:** Can money buy happiness? Yours—or a close friend or loved one? Most think so, especially the young and those who have received lump sums that usually come as gifts or through inheritances. Truth be told, it doesn't last long for many. It's easy to say, "If I only had more income (savings, investments, real estate, etc.), I would be more happy (comfortable, satisfied, joyful, generous, etc.)." Really? Let's find out.

**To Do:** Read the columns below. Circle or underline all the words that most sound like where you are or how you feel today.

# Money $marts Attitude Scale

| 1 | 2 | 3 | 4 | 5 |
|---|---|---|---|---|
| Unhappy | Unproductive | Steady | Happy | Joyful |
| Insecure | Barely Coping | Average | Tension Free | Accomplished |
| Angry | Not good enough | Ordinary | Aspiring | Acknowledged |
| Lonely | Not having enough | OK | Secure | Valued |
| Need Love | Improving | Accepted | Fun | Powerful |
| Inhibited | Searching | Satisfied | Pleased | Confident |
| Unfinished | Making do | Common | Peaceful | Exhilarated |
| Uncomfortable | Struggling | Worthy | Competent | Blissful |
| Disappointed | Need assurance | Likable | Prepared | Excited |
| Fatigued | Tense | Agreeable | Capable | Passionate |
| Low self-esteem | Relationships need improving | Relationship OK | Productive | Making a difference |

Source: © The Briles Group, Inc. 1995

Now, how much income do you have per month— $0 to $1000, $1001 to $2000, $2001 to $3000, $3001 to $4000 or over $4000? If you compared your income and column number with a hundred, even a thousand other people, the result may surprise you. In real life, most people, no matter how much they make, will be to the left of the "Average/Normal" column #3! Are you?

If you are like most, average, it does not mean, "Why bother?" As in, "Why bother to learn or do anything about money if it doesn't impact your comfort level?" Instead, it means there is more to money; money is just a means, not an end in itself. **Money**

**$marts** is about *creating and using money, not loving it.* Money can conceive the security and freedom your family desires to pursue its values and plan for the future. How it grows is up to you. Your money future is the palette from which you choose to paint—as brilliant and diverse or as simple and neutral as you want.

Think of money as a tool. If used and cared for, you have almost unlimited years of service. If neglected or ignored, it rusts and rots away. You are the key ingredient in your money tool kit. How?— by becoming astute as to what makes and what does not make good money smarts. Savings; investing; credit; housing; retirement planning; getting good, solid advice along the way; and everything in between, are all factors in enhancing your money confidence. Without them, you are hampered in your quest to get control of your family finances. The tools you put together will be your magic carpet to financial self-reliance.

 Below, write about how you would like finances to be— think in 5- to 10-year periods.

**I/We want our money palette to look like:**

_____

_____

_____

_____

How important is money to you? How much do you think you need? Write a few sentences about the importance of money to you, and your family, if appropriate. List what you would be willing to give up, as well as what you would not be willing to give up to have "enough" money.

**Give Up:**

_____

_____

_____

_____

**Not Give Up:**

_____

_____

_____

_____

*To Do:* **Identify your Money $marts Persona**

You may ask, "What motivates *me* with my money decisions and habits?" To find out, take the *Money $marts Persona Quiz* below. Instructions for scoring and determining your style follow.

## Money $marts Persona Quiz

1. **Your Aunt Martha dies, leaving you her prized pearls and stocks that have a current market value of $50,000. You—**
   A. Immediately take the stocks to a broker and sell them so that you can buy the things you really want, especially a new wardrobe to go with the pearls.
   B. Get the stock certificates and place them and the pearls in a safe deposit box.
   C. Do nothing.
   D. Sell the stocks and buy shares in companies that you think will double in value within the next few years.
   E. Donate the shares to the Girl Scouts, your favorite non-profit organization.

2. **Your best friend has just filed for bankruptcy. You—**
   A. Advised your friend to charge everything she could on her credit cards before she filed for the bankruptcy.
   B. Know that you don't want it to ever happen to you, that's why you save a lot of everything you get.
   C. Know that no money problem will ever force you to do *that*.
   D. Worry that it could someday happen to you.

E.  Decide that you don't want to be around her as much
    as you have in the past.

**3.  *The bonus you were counting on is only half what you
    expected. You—***

A.  Decide that a shopping spree is in order.

B.  Take back the new outfit you purchased the previous
    week.

C.  Can't tell your spouse how much it is.

D.  Call and see if you can get the deposit back on the new
    car you wanted.

E.  Withdraw, from yourself, and your friends.

**4.  *To be financially comfortable, you—***

A.  Have enough money coming in, therefore comfort is
    just a matter of going to work and doing what you love.

B.  Need to increase your salary and have at least a million
    dollars in savings.

C.  Are not really sure what you need.

D.  Need to pay for everything in cash, including a new car
    and house.

E.  Want to increase your donations to charity.

**5.  *You've just got a credit card offer in the mail. You—***

A.  Apply for anything that comes along, knowing that you
    can meet your monthly payments.

B. Consider it only if it has no annual fee.

C. Toss it in the trash.

D. Put it in a pile of mail to be looked at a later time.

E. Would only consider applying for it if it supports one of your causes.

**6. The stock market keeps going up. You—**

A. Borrow money to invest.

B. Call your broker to cash out.

C. Don't have a clue what "up" means.

D. Sell half of your holdings.

E. You endow a chair at your alma mater with the increased value of your investments.

**7. You are one of the winners in a Power Ball lottery. Your share of the prize is $10,000,000. You—**

A. Quit your job, order a great new chair to watch your new 60-inch flat screen TV, invite 20 of your friends for two weeks in Hawaii on your nickel, and order your dream car.

B. Select the annuity option for the rest of your life.

C. Are shell-shocked and eventually decide to hire a money manager to take over.

D. Tell each member of your immediate family that they can select a special "something," then invest the rest.

E.  Change your name so no one will know of your good
fortune.

**8.  *Your accountant has advised you to get your financial
records in order. You—***

A.  Have always used the shoebox approach and can think
of no reason to take the time to transfer everything
onto a software program for your computer.

B.  Are in your glory. The challenge of the new computer
program fits you to a tee!

C.  Know you will get to it, that's why you save *everything*
in a box somewhere in the basement.

D.  Like to keep track of all the guarantees you have
received over the years, including the tags you tear off
merchandise you buy.

E.  Ignore your accountant . . . that's his job to keep track
of stuff.

**9.  *When I think about a budget, my response is—***

A.  Budget, what's a budget?

B.  It's a good thing.

C.  It's never been a topic of conversation in my household.

D.  I like to tinker with them, especially on the computer.

E.  I take great pride in always living within my means.

**10.  *I worry about money when—***

A.  I don't, I'd rather think of ways to spend it.

B. I'm awake, it's constantly on my mind.

C. Ever I read or hear about financial bad news or I'm in a crisis.

D. I'm not involved in other things that take my mind off of it.

E. Not often, there are other, more important things to worry about.

**Scoring:** The greatest number of a given letter will indicate your money persona. There are pros and cons to each style.

## Who You Are

**A** *Spender* If you have mostly A's, your attitude is "what I have, I will spend." Budgets aren't in your vocabulary; you freely spend money on your friends and you're likely to have credit card debt, which can get you into trouble. The plus is that you aren't held back by money worries and that you are generous, sometimes overly generous. A *Spender* is likely to be the one that reaches for the tab when dining out with friends, much to the chagrin of a partner or spouse.

**B** *Keeper* B's indicate that you fit the common perception of a hoarder. It's very difficult for you to spend anything on anybody, from yourself to the ones you love. The plus is that when money chaos hits the general population, you don't have to worry about taking care of your family. The negative is that *Keepers* often hold back more if times look tough, even when they have what most would view as, plenty of money.

**C**     ***Dodger***     A preference for C statements means that you will do just about anything to avoid a discussion about money, even if it is good news. Deep inside, you feel that you just don't have the skills to handle it. The plus is that you are not obsessed about what money is doing.

**D**     ***Postponer***     When it comes to money, anyone with mostly D statements is inclined to put off spending money whenever possible, no matter how small the amount. Money concerns envelop your thoughts to the point that you can be obsessed with what you perceive as the lack of money even when you have substantial savings. A *Postponer* is not necessarily a *Keeper*, although there are similarities. *Postponers* are willing to spend money, as long as there is backup in savings and investments. *Keepers* don't want to spend, period.

**E**     ***Atoner***     A high number of *E* responses indicates that you may be embarrassed about the money you have, you make or that you come from. Most *Atoners* live fairly uncomplicated and luxury-free lives. If unexpected money is received, it is not uncommon for an *Atoner* to pass it on to a cause. A common attitude is that "I didn't have it before and all was fine, I don't need it now." *Atoners* will rarely replace household items and cars with newer models until they absolutely have to be replaced. Money is rarely wasted.

No matter what your **Money \$marts Persona** is, it doesn't mean that one style is any better than any other, although each impacts what you do with money now and what you will do with it in the future. In reality, a little bit of each makes sense at different times of your money life.

***Money \$marts Tip:*** Abraham Lincoln wrote, "Most people are just about as happy as they make up their minds to be." Part of your money journey will be to discover what you really need for your foundation. When I was a Certified Financial Planner™ Professional, I consistently observed that my most successful clients were not the high earners—they made average incomes. They created plans that fit their life styles and goals. Those who made significant amounts of money usually kept a money banana dangling in front of them—always needing and wanting more.

In the end, it was my school teacher and nurse clients who really did sock money away for their future. A little bit every month—that's how they got started, and it paid off big. By creating a habit that extended over many years, many of them have investments and savings exceeding $1,000,000!

# 2

# Getting Organized

*Planning for your money future begins with planning today.*
*It also includes planning for the unexpected.*

**To Think About:** We are not a paperless society. Most families have junk drawers—the place where you throw all the warranties and miscellaneous documents that you will file "someday." From the time you were a little kid, you probably gathered *stuff*. I bet you have a report card that is several decades old (I do)! Hard to believe, but that's good news. Out of all that paper buried in drawers, boxes and bags are the makings for building your money file system.

Getting organized means that you will know exactly where your old tax returns, mortgage papers, loan applications and payoffs, credit reports, retirement accounts, any investment and bank accounts, car documents, various insurance policies, improvements to your home, warranties, even bills to be paid are! This is one of the major areas where a money cloud can shade a household. *It just seems like so much stuff to keep track of.*

It is. But, you have to. If you don't, chaos continues to be your partner. For you to complete our 30-day "get-our-act-together" program, you need to process through this step. What you find will fill in the blanks in several other spots in this guide. It's the beginning of a true measurement of where you presently are and where you want to arrive.

***To Do:*** You need a place to put the documents you are gathering. Ideally, a small filing cabinet can work wonders, especially when it is accompanied with real files. Manila ones are fine—you may even want to stretch and do a little color coding, either with labels or the actual file (try red for your Action-Problem To Do file). If you don't have a file (or don't want to purchase one), a heavy duty cardboard box from the stationery store works well. The point is to have a receptacle and a regular spot that you will unload your treasures and financial data to. Here's a starting point:

# Money $marts Quick File Method

**Household Files:**

Appliances Info-Warranties

Electronic Info-Warranties

Garage and Outdoor Tools Info-Warranties

Home Furnishings

Other

Other

**Financial Files-Use One for Each Separate Item or Company:**

Automobiles

Bank Accounts

Canceled Checks

Credit Cards

Insurance

Investments

Home Improvements & Repairs

Home Purchase & Sale

Loans

Mortgage

Medical

Real Estate

Retirement Plans

# Money $marts Quick File Method

Trusts, Wills & Estate Plans

Other

Other

## Taxes—Federal & State:

Current Year-Income

Next Year-Income

Previous Years (6)-Income

Real Estate

## Current Bills:

Bills to be Paid

Monthly Files for Bills Already Paid (12)

Action-Problem To Do

## Names, Phone #s and Addresses of All Advisors and Agents

Accountant

Attorney

Financial Planner

Insurance

Family or Friend

Other

Other

Other

Other

Keep separate categories for all your appliance warranties, receipts and general information. Most likely, you may not look at them until something goes wrong or you replace with a newer model. If you own a home, most improvement expenses can be used to offset part of profits when you sell. Use separate files for each credit card.

Within your files, it usually makes sense to have envelopes to separate the various receipts— i.e., personal income tax deductions. You can file receipts as you accumulate them and keep a total monthly (or yearly) total for your tax appointment with your accountant. You need to access tax info anytime you apply for a loan of any sort.

## What to Toss

If you are like most people, you collect stuff. The paper trail is no exception. Here's what to keep:

1  **Investment Information**—you need to know how much you paid for something, how much you sold it for and whether or not you got interest or dividends while you held them. Brokerage firms and mutual fund companies send statements—keep them until you no longer need them and have reported the gain/loss to the IRS. Backup data should be kept for six years with tax return.

**2    Retirement Account and Paycheck Records**—current tax law requires you to keep Forms 1040, 8606, 1099R and 5498 for each year you made a contribution to your IRA. Keep paycheck stubs until you get the W-2 you file with your tax return—toss those if all the numbers in each category add up.

**3    Insurance Policies**—keep copies of all current insurance policies. Once you cancel one, keep a copy for up to two years, then toss.

**4    Medical Records**—current tax law allows you to deduct anything over 7.5% of your AGI (adjusted gross income) on your federal tax return. If your AGI is $40,000, you can deduct expenses in excess of $3,000, excluding medical insurance premiums. If your medical expenses don't exceed 7.5% for your AGI, toss the receipts.

**5    Credit Card Receipts and Statements**—when you receive your monthly statement and all matches up, you can toss the receipt. The exception would be if there is a possibility of needing to replace or return the item or you are dealing with an erroneous charge, keep the receipt. I use a mini-file each year that has monthly tabs and just put them in the monthly slot. If I need to find the receipt, I've found that my memory gives me an estimate of when I bought the item (winter, summertime, etc.), and I can find it quickly.

**6  Canceled Checks and Bank Statements**—keep bank statements for at least six years (IRS may need copies if an audit surfaces). Any ATM receipts should be matched to bank statement, then tossed. Canceled checks relating to home improvement should be kept to support improvements when sold; otherwise, they can be tossed after a year.

**7  Household Bills and Receipts**—food, utilities, etc. are expensive, but not deductible (if you have a home office, get tax advise—some expenses will be deductible). If you pay for child care and education expenses, these amounts will be used on your tax return—so keep them. If you have had a casualty loss related to fires, weather destruction, etc., you may be able to take a deduction. Again, your tax advisor is the best source on what you can and cannot do.

**8  Home Purchase/Sale and Improvements**—presently, if you sell your home and are single, you get up to $250,000 in tax-free profits; $500,000 if married. Whether you are over or under the tax free zone, it makes sense to hold on to anything that reflects a capital improvement (the new porch counts; the snazzy light bulbs don't). Keep your original buy and sell documents indefinitely.

**9  Mortgage and Property Tax Records**—when you file your taxes, you need the info supplied by the mortgage lender as well as property taxes to include under "itemized deductions." Under current law, you can deduct up to $1,100,000 in interest payments as long as the interest is only for up to two homes. If you own a third one, no additional deduction, even if it's under the $1,100,000 amount. Keep this info for at least six years and as long as you own the house(s).

**10    Federal and State Income Tax Returns**—under current law, you can be audited for up to 6 years by the IRS—so 6 years worth is the minimum. If the IRS suspects fraud in any area, it can audit until the cows come home. So, keep your returns and whatever backup supports them in a box for the "just in case."

***Money $marts Tip:***  When you buy a new computer, it most likely comes with money tracking software—either Microsoft Money or Intuit's Quicken. If not already on your computer, purchase one of them. They are fairly inexpensive and true godsends when it comes to gathering data for income tax purposes.

Intuit also publishes Turbotax and Quickbooks—for taxes and general bookkeeping. Newest on the scene is Quickbooks Simple

Start, an excellent tool for a small business and can literally be set up in seconds. All programs are available for under $100 each. Watch for rebate and discount coupons.

Take advantage of Internet banking through your bank. You can easily download your account information, including deposits and checks written directly to the software program you use.

## What Happens if Something Happens to You?

### To Think About:

*Everyone should have a durable power of attorney*—a legal instrument that tells adults who may have to step in on your behalf what you want. Powers of Attorney are needed for the unexpected—accidents, life threatening illnesses, paralyzing strokes and weird events that occur in society that no one wants to happen to them and their loved ones. But, they do happen, and they happen every day.

Consider the news in my morning paper— it's a heartbreaking story of a young mother who went to the hospital to give birth to her second son. Normally, a joyous event for family and friends. This turned into a family feud.

The mother experienced an extremely rare blood problem at

the birth and went into a coma after the doctors pumped over three times her normal blood amount into her via transfusions. The woman went from critical to a vegetative state in a fairly short period of time.

Enter the family. The husband was in shock. They had been married less than a year. He kept praying for a miracle and wanted to keep her alive. Her sisters wanted to pull the plugs and cease tube-feeding her. Eventually the court was involved. The woman was *only* 40 years old. She died after 8 months of being kept alive.

***To Do:*** What should you do? First of all, determine who you truly trust, someone who will act as your "voice" in an emergency—a backup if you can't function, are in an accident or become very ill suddenly. This person can be your spouse, friend, adult child, or a parent. Talk to them about the unexpected. What do you want done to maintain your life? Do everything possible, no expense spared? Pull all the plugs if your medical team declares you in a vegetative state? Somewhere in between? What?

I promise you, they won't relish your discussion, but it's one that you will never regret initiating. Tell them what you want done if you become incapacitated in any way. If they are willing, give them your power of attorney now. In writing. Your age doesn't matter—everyone needs this backup.

## Health Care

For health care, you need a special form. It will vary from state to state. You can drop by any hospital and pick up a healthcare *durable power of attorney* packet that's right for your state. Or you can write to Choice in Dying, 200 Varick Street, 10th floor, New York, NY 10014-4810 or call 800-989-9455 for a packet for your state to be sent to you. It's free. The website is *choices.org*.

It's a good idea to name two stand-ins for you, one may not be around if any accident occurs and a critical decision has to be made. It can be a family or non-family member (and sometimes it's a smart thing to have a non-member involved—when tragedy strikes, emotions ride high).

To avoid any inaction or delay, either one should be able to act alone on your behalf.

A *living will* should also be completed. It expresses what medical treatments you want (and don't want) in case of a life-threatening emergency. You can find information online, pick up forms in a stationery store, hire an attorney to draw one up, even buy a book to help you out. If married or have a partner, he or she should do the same.

Make sure your personal physician, spouse and family members know what your druthers are. Give a copy to each of your signed documents and any time you make changes, update copies to them as well.

If you aren't sure what you want done if you become incapacitated, you can create a *springing power of attorney*. It only comes
to life if you become disabled and can't act for yourself. Your
springing power of attorney will define what that means. It will
read something like this:

> I shall be deemed disabled when two physicians licensed to
> practice medicine in my state sign a document stating that I am
> disabled and unable to handle my personal affairs. If this hap-
> pens, John Maling, my husband, will handle my affairs. When
> two physicians licensed to practice medicine in my state sign a
> document stating that I am able to handle my affairs again,
> John Maling will no longer serve as my power of attorney.

A durable power of attorney is really another form of insurance and
should be reviewed every four to five years. If you decide that you
want to change it, including the person who would act on your
behalf, inform them, both verbally and in writing. Destroy whatever copies you had made previously and substitute new ones.

***Money $marts Tip:*** Hospitals routinely request that
you complete a durable power of attorney if you are
admitted. This is one of the records that you want to review annually to make sure it says exactly what your intent is.

# 3 Credit. . . Friend or Foe?

*Recklessness with credit can cost a mini-fortune.*

**To Think About:** Americans owe more money than any other western civilization! We get deeper into debt every year. In the last decade, Americans charged more than 1 trillion dollars on their cards. More than $973 billion is owed in credit card balances, with the average household carrying more than $9,200 in credit card debt alone.

A credit card is used over 600 times every second of the day; over 36,000 times a minute; over 2 million times an hour; over 52 million times a day.

You may be one of the few who really do pay off every credit card in full every month before the due date. Even if that's the case, do not skip this chapter. Why? Because, errors are made. Not in you paying your bills. But in the way your creditors report your bill-paying habits to the credit reporting agencies.

Two-thirds of the entries will contain some type of error. Mistakes include wrong balances, erroneous payment dates, even liens and collections reported that may belong to Sam or Samantha Johnson instead of Samuel and Susie Johnson (that's you in this example). The end result is that it dings you if you apply for credit from anyone who checks your credit and receives the wrong information.

You may think, "No big deal, I'll just call and tell the credit reporting agency to fix their files." If it were only that easy. It's not. Weeks, even months go by before anything is "fixed." Lo and behold, years can elapse, and the same error is resurrected!

Think slooooooooooow when attempting to straighten credit misinformation out. With the rapidly evolving cyberworld, it's most likely that errors will continue to compound. Better to keep the error from happening in the first place!

## Ignorance Is Not Bliss

Too many don't know what their credit score means. A survey by the Consumer Federation of America showed that only one-third correctly understood that credit scores indicate the risk of not repaying a loan (which also means credit card debt).

Today, credit reports are used for purposes beyond borrowing. Everyone from utility companies, landlords, auto insurance companies even employers. The U.S. Public Interest Research Group found that an appalling 79% of reports had errors in them in 2004. On top of that, it found that 25% of the errors would have resulted in a denial of credit. That's huge!

Having a low credit score means you pay more money in interest charges. How does that compute?

Consider this—if you had a FICO score (Fair, Issac & Company, *MyFico.com*) of 720 or above (excellent), a $150,000 30-year mortgage could have a 5.72% interest rate or $872 monthly payment. If your score is low, say 560, you will be looking at a 9.29% interest rate. The monthly payment will be $1,238 or a $4,400 annual difference in mortgage payments—that's significant money!

Below is a 30-year $200,000 loan broken out with interest rates, interest paid, monthly payment, FICO score ranges and the increased amount you would have to pay when your FICO score is reduced.

Automotive and credit card loans work the same way. The higher the FICO score you have, the lower the interest rate you will be charged. The easiest way to increase your FICO score is to pay your bills on time and reduce outstanding balances.

## Cost of $200,000 Loan

| FICO Score | Interest Rate | Monthly Payment | Total Interest Paid | Increased Interest Paid |
|---|---|---|---|---|
| 720-850 | 5.501% | $1,136 | $208,853 | |
| 700-719 | 5.626% | $1,151 | $214,518 | = $ 5,665 |
| 675-699 | 6.163% | $1,220 | $239,250 | = $ 30,397 |
| 620-674 | 7.313% | $1,373 | $294,247 | = $ 85,394 |
| 560-619 | 8.531% | $1,542 | $355,200 | = $146,347 |
| 500-559 | 9.289% | $1,651 | $394,362 | = $185,509 |

## Identity Theft Is Huge

Identity theft is the fastest growing consumer scam. It costs banks and other financial institutions billions of dollars each year. Twenty percent of the population is dealing with some form of this problem. The first sign often comes with a rejection of a credit request—yours.

Reports of delinquencies, non-payments, bill collectors, even too much credit will reduce your score. If you are the target of identity theft, expect to spend huge amounts of time in trying to correct it—and money; if you need legal help in correcting the credit records, you could easily spend $10,000. When identity theft occurs, it takes the average consumer a minimum of six months to unravel. And still, it's probable that you will be stuck with bad credit for several years.

Dealing with credit requires that you find out what the credit reporting agencies are telling other potential creditors about you. Incorrect information in your credit file is one of the single biggest culprits of creating money chaos in your life and the number one complaint from consumers to the Federal Trade Commission.

Expect to spend a lot of time unraveling mistakes you uncover. That's why checking on what the credit bureaus have in their records is a critical factor in having money smarts. Do it twice a year. Start digging—it's really pretty simple to get the ball rolling.

**To Do:** Get out paper and pen and call or write to the three major credit reporting agencies—*Experian, TransUnion* and *Equifax*. Or, go to their websites. Since 2004, you no longer had to pay to get a copy of your report—you can get one from each of the major reporting agencies once a year. More often than that, you may have to pay.

The exception is that if you have been denied credit for anything in the past 60 days and you have the denial letter, the agency that is identified on the letter will send you a copy free.

Your letter should be very brief. Merely state your name (include initials); if married, your spouse's name; current address and if you

lived there less than five years, your former address and your
Social Security number. Sign your letter. Include your denial letter (remember, it's free when credit is denied even if you already
received your one free copy from each).

Experian    800-397-3742
*Experian.com*
PO Box 9532
Allen, TX 75013

TransUnion    800-680-7289
*TUC.com*
PO Box 6790
Fullerton, CA 92834

Equifax    800-525-6285
*Equifax.com*
PO Box 740241
Atlanta, GA 30374

You can also hit the Internet. Go to *AnnualCreditReport.com* and
request yours. The site will ask for personal information to make
sure you are really you requesting your report. As soon as the
report appears on the screen, print it immediately. If you close it,

your free report is no longer free. You will have to pay to get another copy.

Now, wait for their responses. It could take a few weeks. By the time they arrive, you have gotten your financial records together and will be able to tell if anyone else's debts are being reported on yours. If they are, your job will be to immediately contact the credit reporting agency and dispute the item.

Once you get your reports and note any discrepancies, the agencies have 45 days to fix the problem after you notify them. With the identify theft problems, request that your credit report no longer include the first five digits of your Social Security number. It's a start.

If your credit report comes back accurate, don't assume it will always be. It is wise to check into what is being reported once a year, just as you do with an annual physical checkup. Any time you apply for a mortgage, request your FICO score from the lender. This will become part of your annual fiscal checkup.

***Money Smarts Tip:*** If you plan to apply for a loan, credit card, a new job or life insurance anytime soon, you definitely want to know what is in your file. If there are errors, and they are uncorrected, you may be rejected and not know why. Once rejected, it's difficult to reverse. You can learn more about disputing information on your credit reports at two websites: *FTC.gov/credit* and *ConsumersUnion.org*.

***To Do:*** If you have credit cards that carry balances, get them out of your wallet now. Call the customer service phone number on the card and say something like this—

> "Over the past month, I've received several offers to transfer my account balances to another credit card company at a much lower interest rate. What will you REDUCE my interest rate to if I retain my account with you?" In 60-70% of your calls, the customer service rep will reduce the rate by several points.

If you are told that the rep isn't authorized to reduce the interest rate you are being charged, say something like this—

> "I know that if I transfer my balance and close the account, your bank is going to mail me an offer for another card with a lower interest rate."

If the rep continues to resist, ask to speak to the supervisor. Repeat the request.

If you succeed in dropping the interest rate, bravo—this is found money that can be used to reduce balances. If you don't succeed, even after threatening to close the account, transfer the balance to a card with a lower rate. If you have had the credit card that you are transferring the balance from for a few years, don't close it . . . just don't use it. Why?—for some reason, FICO will ding you for closing an account that has a history to it—better to tuck it in a drawer or deep freeze it.

To find what the current lowest rates are, go to *BankRate.com* and *CardWeb.com*. To find your FICO score, go to *MyFico.com*.

***Money $marts Tip:*** To find the right credit card for you—from debit cards to award cards, go to *Credit-Cards.com*. Pros and cons of each will be disclosed, what the true costs are, how to qualify, etc. Other websites you should check out include *BankRate.com, CardRatings.com* and *CardWeb.com.*

**Order your reports today . . . Credit will be revisited later in the month.**

# 4 Your Net Worth—The Tool for Measurement

*Growth always involves some risk.*

 **To Think About:** One of your first steps in developing your **Money $marts** profile is to determine what your net worth is. It will become the basis for checking your pulse on how you are doing. You do this by adding up your assets and subtracting your debits and liabilities. *The result is your net worth.*

Ideally, your assets are of greater value than your liabilities. If they aren't, don't give up. You, and your family, will always be the single best asset you have. It will be your ability and efforts that will create your future *positive net worth.* Your material assets may be on the lean side today; next year, the picture can be totally different. The deciding factor will depend on what you do over the remaining 30 days and the rest of the year. Your net worth has two components: the material side—assets minus liabilities— and the emotional side.

It's usually straightforward to gauge the material side; it's the emotional side's components that are more difficult to weigh, if not impossible. Between partners, spouses and within families, risk-taking attitudes and abilities may be on opposite ends of the spectrum.

An investment option may be fine and comfortable for you . . . and give your partner nightmares. The key is to identify these differences and discuss them openly. You may need to avoid some areas when it comes to investments. You both need to determine if any fears or concerns are valid. If they are, can they be overcome or modified to satisfy you both?

***To Do:*** The only way to create a net worth statement is to do one. You can copy one from the zillions of financial planning and money workbooks in book stores today, by getting a blank loan application or using the *Money $marts Quick Net Worth Statement* below. Whichever method you choose, the important thing is to do it now. Most of the information that you need to fill in the blanks below has already been gathered during the preceding days.

You will need to know the values of any investments and retirement plans that you own and participate in. Don't use the new car value for cars—figure a minimum reduction of 20% value when you drove off the lot.

The value of your home is what you could sell it for today, not what you bought it for. With the Internet, you can look up recent sales of properties in your neighborhood. Or, ask a trusted Realtor®.

Investments, art, antiques and jewelry values are the amount you can get for them if you sold today. Take the latest statement values for bank, savings and any insurance accounts.

Your various debt balances would be what the account balance is as of today—your loan and credit card statements all reflect outstanding balances.

| Money $marts Quick Net Worth Statement |
|---|
| **ASSETS—What You Own** |
| Bank Accounts: |
|     Checking |
|     Savings |
|     CDs/Time Deposits |
|     Money Market Accounts |
| Insurance Cash Values |
| Investments: |
|     Bonds |
|     Mutual Funds |
|     Stocks |
|     Rental Property |
|     Other |
| Money Owed You |
| Retirement Plans |
|     Annuities |

# Money $marts Quick Net Worth Statement

Pensions

401(k) or 403(b)

Social Security

Residence

Cars

Antiques, Artwork, Jewelry

Personal Property

Other

Other

Other

**TOTAL ASSETS** (add all of the above assets)

**LIABILITIES—What You Owe**

Credit Cards

Mortgage(s)

Car Loans

Student Loans

Other

Other

Other

**TOTAL LIABILITIES** (add all of the above liabilities)

**NET WORTH** (total assets minus total liabilities)

***Money $marts Tip:*** You will be asked to complete a financial statement any time you apply for a loan. So, make it a habit that you revisit annually. With money software, all you need to do is the initial input, then an annual update to it to keep it current. All you need to do is print it out.

# 5 Where Does Your Money Go?

*Everything costs more when you don't have any money.*

 **To Think About:** You may think there is a money sink hole out there. Your money just disappears, usually never to be seen or heard from again. It doesn't matter if you are single, with just you to be accountable to, or if you have a spouse and kids.

Do you write checks for everything? Do you like the feel of the green stuff, paying cash for everything from entertainment, eating out, clothes and gasoline? Do you try to charge everything on your credit card(s)? Or, do you hit the ATM whenever you need cash, not using checks or credit cards?

Today, we are not throwing the "B" word at you yet. Budgets and Spending Plans will surface soon enough. The reality is that you can't do any planning until you know what you do with the money you already get. If you are a saver, others in your family may not be. After all, we dance to different drummers. The money dance is no different.

### *To Think About:* **ATM Money: Now You See It, Now You Don't**

When I worked with clients, the topic of cash flow . . . or lack of it. . . almost always surfaced. Money ran out before the end of the month . . . and no one knew where it went!

Guess what—I knew where it went, and I bet you do too. Modern technology has two faces: simplicity and convenience. Welcome to the world of ATMs—those windows that spew out 20 dollar bills right and left—the Automatic Teller Machines. When my kids were young, they thought as long as I had blank checks in my check book, there was money. Today's kids think that as long as the ATM is at every corner, money is bountiful. Unfortunately, so do too many ATM users.

Most ATMs require that you withdraw a minimum amount— usually it's $20. As you approach your conveniently placed ATM, you might wonder, "Is $20 enough? Maybe I should get $40 or $100 to tide me through the weekend." This might sound like a good idea. Maybe, maybe not.

When money is unaccounted for, the most probable use of it is for purchasing an impulse item. What's an impulse item?—how about a frozen yogurt, a latte, a magazine, a movie or a tall lemonade on a hot day? These items range from a dollar here to several dollars there. Before you can say, "Automatic Teller

Machine," your cash has gone "poof." Ah, but you are thinking, "I can always go back and get some more."

Right. And wrong. These very convenient items get a lot of people into trouble. My experience is that 1) many forget to enter the withdrawal in their checkbook register and 2) most take more than what they actually need . . . and spend it all. Once cash goes into a pocket, wallet or purse, it just disappears. You can't remember where it was spent; it was just spent. It's gone to cash heaven!

If your money is evaporating and you are having a hard time tracking where your money goes, immediately stop using your ATM card. Put it in the freezer and forget about it. Write checks for everything, even $1.50 if the merchant will take it. Why?— because now you have a written track record of where and what you spent your money on. Some banks charge a fee—ouch!

"What—give up my cash card?" Yes, indeed. "But," you say, "I work and I can't bank during regular hours." Wrong. What's regular? Today, banking hours range from 7 a.m. to 6 p.m. and Saturdays to boot.

The bottom line is this: ATM cards are real culprits when it comes to money problems. Unless you really track where your cash goes, you are not prone to impulse buying and spending, and your cash does not run out before the end of the month, my advice is to trash the card.

***To Do:*** So, where does your money go each day—week—month? Let's find out. Beginning today, every member in your family becomes a sleuth. Every dollar, dime and penny is tracked for the remainder of your **Money $marts** month. If you already know the amounts spent the previous four days, great, include them. Ideally, this exercise needs to be done for an entire quarter so that all expenditures are included, such as quarterly insurance payments.

Get an inexpensive spiral pad or notebook and label pages for different items—meals out (note which meal it is), clothing, sundries, insurances, car and transportation expenses, groceries, entertainment, credit card and debt payments (not mortgage), household repairs and maintenance, mortgage or rent, gifts, healthcare, utilities, savings, taxes (don't forget to count the amounts withheld from paychecks), child care, child support, alimony, educational, pets and of course, investments, retirement, and other.

Don't forget to include a category for unaccountable cash—it happens. As you do this, you will probably come up with a few categories of your own. Duplicate the sections below as needed.

# Money $marts Sleuthing Cash Flow Statement

## Money That You Pay Out – FIXED:

Alimony/Spousal Maintenance

Car Payment #1

Car Payment #2

Child Care

Child Support

Clothing

Common Charges (condo/association fees)

Credit Card Payment #1

Credit Card Payment #2

Credit Card Payment #3

Credit Card Payment #4

Credit Card Payment #5

Credit Card Payment #6

Credit Card Payment #7

Loan Payment #1

Loan Payment #2

Loan Payment #3

Student Loan Payment

Insurance - Car

Insurance – Homeowner/Renter

# Money $marts Sleuthing Cash Flow Statement

| |
|---|
| Insurance - Health |
| Insurance - Life |
| Insurance - Disability |
| Internet - Cable |
| Health Club Membership |
| Household Repairs & Maintenance |
| Health Care – Doctors |
| Health Care – Prescriptions |
| Housekeeper |
| Mortgage or Rent |
| Parking Expenses for Work |
| Phone – Land line |
| Phone - Cell |
| Retirement Accounts |
| Savings |
| School – College Tuition |
| School – Private |
| School – Tutoring |
| Summer Camp Tuition |
| Taxes |
| Transportation (other than car) |

# Money $marts Sleuthing Cash Flow Statement

| | |
|---|---|
| Utilities-Gas/Electric | |
| Yard Work | |
| Other | |
| **Total FIXED Cash Out** | |
| | |
| **Money That You Pay Out – OTHER/VARIABLE:** | |
| Books | |
| CDs – Music – Videos – DVDs | |
| Cigarettes - Cigars - Liquor | |
| Clothing | |
| Coffee | |
| Dry Cleaning | |
| Entertainment - In | |
| Entertainment - Out | |
| Investments | |
| Gifts | |
| Groceries | |
| Grooming (Haircuts, Manicures, Pedicures) | |
| Newspapers, Magazines | |
| Pets (Food, Grooming) | |
| Snacks | |

| **Money $marts Sleuthing Cash Flow Statement** |
| --- |
| Stuff for House (pots, towels, plants, etc.) |
| Stuff for Grooming (shampoo, lotion, etc.) |
| Takeout – Dinner, Lunch, Breakfast |
| Vacation & Trips |
| Veterinary |
| Other |
| Other |
| Other |
| Other |
| Unaccountable Cash |
| **Total OTHER/VARIABLE Cash Out** |

At the end of the day, a designated family member inputs everyone's expenditures. If you have older kids, 11 and up, this is a great exercise in creating awareness of just how much it costs to operate your household.

Finally, total both sections. You will use these numbers to determine if you are over (spending more money than you have coming in) or under (you spend less money than what you receive monthly). Transpose your Fixed Costs and Other Costs. You end up with a "TaDah!"—Total Money Out.

| Total **FIXED** Costs | |
| --- | --- |
| Total **OTHER/VARIABLE** Costs | |
| **TOTAL MONEY OUT** | |

### Kick the Habit

Everyone has a few bad habits. Which do you have and what do they cost? Think about smoking, beer and wine out with pals, lattes and "designer" coffee and teas, movie tickets, fast food, bagels, muffins and doughnuts, meals out, magazines at the checkout stand at the grocery, even lottery tickets. Think of all the goodies that you spend money on that could be classified as "impulse" buys. You want it . . . but do you need it?

I know, I know—this activity can be a real pain in the neck. It takes time—something you probably don't have in abundance. But, it is critical and needs to be done every day. If you skip it, you will sabotage all your efforts to get control of your family finances.

 ***Money $marts Tip:*** If you have a computer and don't use a personal finance program such as Quicken, this is a good time to invest in one. The full retail cost is approximately $80—with the rebates that are normally offered, you will get it for under $50. These programs are not complicated; they help you keep track of balances and your spending; they create Spending Plans, aka budgets; they track investments, and can even pay bills; and help with long term planning. In other words, they are a welcome addition to your financial independence.

## 6

# Income Sources

*Don't ignore the small change, it adds up.*

**To Think About:** Identifying where income comes from is a lot easier than probing where it goes. Do you ever think in terms of "gross" income versus "net" income? Your paycheck is a good example. Gross is what you start with before all the deductions are taken—federal and state taxes, Social Security (FICA), contributions to charitable causes such as United Way, healthcare insurance, retirement accounts, loan payments and savings payments. You may have other deductions.

What's left over is the net amount you usually deposit into your checking account. The amount that you have to pay for all the other items that you need and want.

It is not unusual to ignore all the withholdings that normally occur. You may be surprised to find that you really don't know why certain amounts are being withheld or what percentage they represent of your monthly gross income. Now's the time to find out.

*To Do:* Get your paycheck stubs for the last month. Most companies routinely detail the amounts withheld each pay period on an accompanying stub. Each pay period should show an accumulated amount from the preceding period.

| **TOTAL Income from Salary(s)** |
| --- |
| How much is withheld for taxes? |
| How much is withheld for retirement purposes? |
| How much is deducted for other purposes? |
| **TOTAL Amount Withheld** |
| **NET Money Available**<br>(total salary minus withheld) |

*To Do:* Apart from your salary, what other sources of income do you have? Categories such as gifts, inheritances, trusts, investments, savings, money market funds, annuities, capital gains, dividends, interest, bonuses, retirement and pension accounts, rental property, refunds and selling stuff you don't want or need all come to mind.

Identify your other sources of money:

| Other Income Sources | |
|---|---|
| 1 | |
| 2 | |
| 3 | |
| 4 | |
| 5 | |
| **TOTAL Other Income Sources** | |

From the preceding day, you've identified where money goes.

| | |
|---|---|
| Total FIXED Costs | |
| Total OTHER/VARIABLE Costs | |
| **TOTAL MONEY OUT** | |
| | |
| Total INCOME Sources | |
| DIFFERENCE Over (+) or Under (-) | |

## Pennies, Nickels and Dimes Can Be Your Best Friends

Never underestimate the value of a few cents here and a few cents there. I keep an old plastic peanut jar in my closet. Its job is to be the collection site of all the change that comes into the house. Sometimes, I add paper money to the jar as a "kicker." At the end of the month, it's tallied and deposited to savings (or to a mutual fund account)—anywhere from $50 to $150 gets added to the kitty. If I had kept those coins in my purse or pocket, it would have been spent. This way it becomes part of the savings plan. To me, it's found money, a real bonus.

***Money $marts Tip:*** Revisit your Fixed and VARIABLE expenses. If your have less money coming in than what goes out, it's time to look closely at the essentials and non-essentials. Many of the items that are listed in the FIXED table on Day 5 can be eliminated—this is the time to ask, "What do I need?" Your answer will most likely be significantly different from "What do I want?"

# 7 Uncle Sam and You

*Pay your taxes, but only what's owed when it's owed.*

**To Think About:** Most people pay more taxes than they owe . . . and they pay them before they are due! This doesn't sound like fun, yet it is repeated in millions of households annually. In the old days (the 80's), if you received a refund after you filed your annual federal tax return, the IRS would send you a notice. It suggested that you change your withholding status to declare more withholding allowances. Why?—because you would reduce or possibly eliminate a refund the following year.

What a novel idea. Get your money back within each paycheck so that you can save, invest, earn interest, pay off bills or spend it! Today, the IRS no longer notifies you that it would be a good idea to *not* receive a refund. After all, it is getting an interest-free loan from the taxpayer—you.

***To Do:*** Enough—it's time to halt the practice. You need to get over *refunditis,* a chronic condition that afflicts millions daily. Do not think of refunds as a savings account—savings accounts pay interest. Refunds don't. If you do get refunds, your homework will be to increase your withholding declarations (allowances) when you go into work tomorrow. If you basically have withheld what you owe at year end, do a spot check to make sure you are on target for the current year and claiming all your deductions. Just like an annual checkup—instead of a physical, you'll do a fiscal one.

The magic form that calculates what you should declare is **Form W-4**—every payroll department has them. If you are self-employed, you can even download from the Internet at *IRS.gov.*

There's a variety of financial data and information that you will need to complete one. Included are:

- The number of dependents you will claim (self, spouse, kids, anyone you contribute over 50% of living costs to— pets don't count). If you and your spouse both work for pay, then decide how you want to divvy up dependents.
- The gross amount you will contribute to retirement accounts, including (401(k)s, 403(b)s, IRAs, SEP-IRAs, KEOGHs, tax sheltered annuities or any other retirement accounts that are available to you.

- Your total deductions that will be listed on your taxes will include:
    - ✔ health care costs—include insurance premiums that are not reimbursed by employers that are in excess of 7.5% of your adjusted gross income (that's the number that includes all your taxable income sources minus retirement contributions, allowable moving expenses, alimony paid, and any penalties on early withdrawal of savings),
    - ✔ mortgage interest,
    - ✔ points deductible for new mortgage loans,
    - ✔ real estate and state taxes,
    - ✔ educational costs that enhance your present job,
    - ✔ investment and accounting expenses,
    - ✔ investment losses (limited to a net $3,000 per year),
    - ✔ losses due to theft and disasters,
    - ✔ donations to charities,
    - ✔ moving costs ( your move must be at least 50 miles' distance from your old job and house),
    - ✔ non-reimbursed job related expenses, and
    - ✔ mandatory uniforms.

Last year's tax return will help as a guide. You must ask this question—Is anything going to change this year?—such as, are we going to buy a new home (mortgage interest is now deductible versus rent not being), have a bigger mortgage or contribute more money to a 401(k) or 403(b)? This is the time you get to roll up your sleeves and guesstimate. Identify:

- Any alimony or spousal support (not child support) paid
- Any interest, dividend, capital gains in excess of losses
- Any taxable pension or retirement distributions received
- Any child care expenses

Using a calculator is a must. If you have a computer, you can purchase a tax program—Turbo Tax is a common tax software program that is fairly easy to use. Tax software is programmed to ask you the questions posed above. With all these numbers, you are ready to tackle the **Form W-4**. It is only two pages, and believe-it-or-not, understandable! Or, complete the new one at your payroll department—don't forget to make a copy for your records.

With **Form W-4** and your totals in hand, you will arrive at the number of allowances you should be declaring within ten minutes. Withholding is more than just you, your spouse and your kids. Every time you have $3,500 in excess deductions, increase your withholding allowance declarations. But, if you claim over 10, you may hear from the IRS, as in, why are you doing this?

Return a letter with their query (if it comes) and explain that you are eliminating the refund you would get the next year because of your allowable deductions, and then identify them, such as the purchase of a home that now has deductible interest and the approximate amount.

Make sure you include a copy of your **Form W-4**. It's rare that you will have a challenge from the IRS.

***Money $marts Tip:*** Congratulations! With the extra monthly money, do one of three things. Pay down any credit card debt first (pay down the ones with the highest interest rate first), then save or invest your new-found money.

One other thought . . . tax information is always guaranteed to change. With the **Form W-4**, amounts for personal allowances will change, sometimes annually. To verify the most current rate, just go to the IRS.gov website and download this year's form.

# Part II
## Developing Your Plan

## (Days 8 – 11)

# 8

# Your Money $marts Goals

*Goals come true when you write them down.*

**To Think About:** Even if you haven't put your money goals down in writing, the odds are that you have spoken them. To your spouse, parents, kids, friends, neighbors, even the cat! And, of course, to yourself. Goals pop out in various ways. As simple as, "When I retire, I'm going to get a cottage on the lake." "When the kids graduate, I'm going to start attending classes." "I'm tired . . . I just want to slow down for awhile."

Sounds grand. How are you going to pay for that cottage or those classes? Your money goals are tangible. You can talk about them and write about them. Have you thought about writing down your goals so you can plan for "whatever" by saving and investing the money you will need?

 **To Do:** Kids often tell you what they want. It's your turn. What do you and your partner/spouse want 5, 10, 15 or

20-plus years from now? What kind of goals would you pursue if you had a magic wand? Think education (for you and/or your kids), retirement nest eggs, housing, a new career or travel. Let your imagination take you on a journey and explore "what if" scenarios. Take turns and write down your wants, hopes and dreams. When you write them out, they have a far greater probability of happening.

## Money $marts Goal Setting

### *You:*

In 5 years, my goals are

_____

_____

_____

In 10 years, my goals are

_____

_____

_____

In 15 years, my goals are

_____

_____

_____

In 20-plus years, my goals are

_____

_____

_____

## *Partner/Spouse:*

In 5 years, my goals are

_____

_____

_____

In 10 years, my goals are

_____

_____

_____

In 15 years, my goals are

_____

_____

_____


In 20-plus years, my goals are

_____

_____

_____


## What do you both want in 5, 10, 15 or 20-plus years?

In 5 years, our goals are

_____

_____

_____


In 10 years, our goals are

_____

_____

_____

In 15 years, our goals are

_____

_____

_____

In 20-plus years, our goals are

_____

_____

_____

Bravo—you've taken the first step—you have identified your goals and put them in writing. Now, how are you going to pay for them? Do you have any idea how much money you will need to underwrite your goals? Few have unlimited bank accounts. If you don't, it merely means that you will start to include savings and investing as a regular part of your monthly spending plan (Spending Plans are introduced tomorrow).

Start estimating what your goals will cost. Begin this process by checking the current cost of whatever the goal or item is (public libraries are great resources—and, don't forget the Internet). Then, factor in an increase for its future purchase based on past inflation data (again, the library and Internet are your allies).

***Money $marts Tip:*** A final word—Don't forget that there are always obstacles before and over the horizon. The best laid plans get diverted. Along with annually revisiting net worth and cash flow statements, it makes good **Money $marts** to revisit your goals. Your attitudes and desires may change. What seems imperative today may be insignificant 5 years from now.

# 9 Spending Plans That Work

*When you focus on "needs" vs. "wants"—you stay in balance.*

**To Think About:** Most people cringe when they hear the "B" word—budget. It's like a diet, not a lot of fun and sure to have restrictions. Let's rename budgets and call them *Spending Plans*. Spending Plans usually address problem areas where cutbacks are needed as well as allocations for spending money. They also include plans for saving and investing.

On Day 5, you started to track where your money was going. Any surprises starting to surface yet? Are you spending more money in some areas than you thought you were? As you continue with your sleuthing, the most likely areas that you will find problems in—also known as over-spending—are: frequent meals out, convenience foods, entertainment, clothing, gifts and cards, vacations (once you are there, credit cards get maxed), and cash taken from the ATM.

***To Do:*** Once you pull money from the ATM, it seems to go to cash heaven! Most people don't have a clue what they did with ATM cash; it just disappears. If you think you have disappearing cash, *immediately stop using your ATM card . . .* don't even wait for your **Money $marts** month to end. ATM usage is one of the biggest culprits in the misuse of money. Look around you. Of all the items in your house, which are necessities and which are just nice to have?

- Take an **Inventory** in your house of all the items you routinely buy in the store to replace when used. Bathrooms, kitchen, garage, yard—everywhere. Don't forget magazines, newspapers, even fresh flowers.
- On a piece of paper, make two columns: **Wants** and **Needs**.
- Each member of the household writes down in either of the columns what he or she believes each item to be: a "want" or a "need." This assumes they are old enough to understand what a "want" and "need" are—wants being a soda versus a glass of water, for example.
- Compare lists. Duplicates in **Needs** should become the first bought when money is available. **Wants** can be deferred, even eliminated, if they don't fit your goals.

***To Do:*** On Day 6, you identified your various income sources. You are now in the process of identifying where all your money goes each month. You have just tallied up the items that are necessities and those that are or would be nice to have. You are now ready to write a *Spending Plan*.

## Money $marts Monthly Spending Plan

**A Fixed Expenses** (payments for the same amount paid monthly):

| |
|---|
| Car |
| Insurance |
| Loans |
| Mortgage or Rent |
| Retirement Accounts |
| Savings |
| Taxes |
| Other |
| Other |
| Other |

**A TOTAL Fixed Expenses**

**B Flexible Expenses** (necessities that vary monthly and annually):

| |
|---|
| Food |
| Charity/Church |

# Money $marts Monthly Spending Plan

| | |
|---|---|
| Clothing | |
| Credit Cards | |
| Healthcare not covered by insurance | |
| Investing | |
| Laundry/Dry cleaning/Cleaning | |
| Personal grooming | |
| Transportation (other than your car) | |
| Other | |
| Other | |
| Other | |
| **B TOTAL Flexible Expenses** | |
| **C Discretionary Spending** (all the things you want): | |
| Eating out | |
| Entertainment | |
| Gifts | |
| Vacations | |
| Other | |
| Other | |
| Other | |
| **C TOTAL Discretionary Spending** | |
| **D TOTAL of all Spending (A+B+C=D)** | |
| **E TOTAL Income Sources from Day 6** | |
| **F Amount of Income** | |
| **OVER or <UNDER> Spending (E-D)** | |

***Money $marts Tip:*** Do you spend over or under your monthly income? Either way, probe your Discretionary and Flexible Spending habits. If your goals are to build a nest egg for college, retirement, a new home or to eliminate debt, prioritizing is essential. Any time you spend money, ask yourself, do I/we need this . . . or do I/we want it? If it doesn't fit into your goals, take a pass.

# 10 To Bank . . . or Not to Bank

*Banks aren't always your best financial friend.*

***To Think About:*** Few people are as loyal to their bank as your parents were. They had their checking, savings, home and car loans all under one roof. They probably got a free toaster along the way. Your generation has a different perspective of what a bank is and is not. Take loans and savings.

Loans are shopped—the borrower is looking for the best rate. Money market funds pay higher rates than most CDs with terms less than 5 years and the car dealership may have better financing for your next car. Car manufacturers and airlines have their own Visa and MasterCard that allow you to accumulate points for purchasing their products or travel services. In the past, banks used to offer better financing. No longer. The question becomes, do you need a bank *and* a banker?

The answer is yes to both. Most likely, you use banks for only a couple of reasons—an all purpose checking account and access to the ATM. If you have an immediate need for a quick loan, your banker may be the person who can give an instant affirmative response. That usually happens only when you have built up a relationship with him or her and the banker knows who you are. Take the time to bypass the drive-in window and actually go in, say hello and introduce yourself.

***To Do:*** Bank charges and rates vary from bank to bank. Determine if you are getting the best possible rates on your checking and any savings accounts. Ask:

- ✔ What does your bank charge for ATM usage and transfer of funds from one account to another?
- ✔ Does it require a minimum balance in order to waive any monthly fees or earn interest on balances?
- ✔ Does the bank put "holds" on checks? Many put an automatic hold on out-of-state checks . . . usually for far more days that it takes the actual check to clear. That means that the bank uses your money when you can't. Not a good thing.
- ✔ If you have multiple accounts, some banks allow you to "link" accounts to meet balance requirements. Does yours?
- ✔ Does your bank accept automatic deposits of paychecks from employers? Does your employer do direct deposits?

Some banks will waive minimum balance requirements if there are automatic deposits by employers.

✔ Does your bank require a high balance ($1000 or more) to receive interest on your balance? Avoid any accounts that require high balances. You are better off using money market funds which are discussed on Day 15.

✔ How does your bank calculate your minimum balance to qualify for a free checking account? Avoid a bank that uses a method called "minimum daily balance." This means that you must keep the minimum balance every single day to qualify. If you drop below the minimum balance just one day, you are charged a fee.

✔ How many checks a month do you write? If you only write a few, ask if it has special accounts (meaning less costly) for someone who writes a few checks a month (such as 10) or for senior citizens.

✔ Online banking and bill paying has finally gained acceptance. Does yours charge for the service? This is an area you might be able to negotiate a bit.

Now, take the above questions and ask your bank's competition the same. You are shopping. You need a bank-type institution for basic money needs. Your goal should be to get the best services for the least amount of money.

*Money $marts Tip:* Banks want your business. The question is: Do you want theirs? By making a few phone calls, you can save several hundred dollars a year in excess fees, charges and lost interest on your money. That's worth an hour or two of your time.

# 11 Borrowing for Today . . . and Tomorrow

*Wanting it all carries a hefty price tag.*

**To Think About:** It is so easy to get stuff today. And, there is so much stuff to get . . . which can be a very bad thing!

The Baby Boom generation has been credited with everything from birthing the term "workaholics" to creating credit cards. Have you ever thought that one of the reasons the older generations have less debt is that they had fewer temptations for their dollars? It's hard to believe that the generation presently collecting Social Security didn't have the use of credit cards when they were young adults.

When you borrow, you are getting today what you will pay for with future income. For that privilege, you pay interest based on the amount initially borrowed, the length of the loan, and whether or not the loan is secured. When you use a credit card, you are getting a loan from the credit card company.

There are times when borrowing makes good **Money $marts**.

Buying a home is at the top of the list—who has all the cash to pay for it up front in full? Formal education is costing more and more. Seventy-five percent of all college educations receive some type of financial aid, including student loans.

In today's highly competitive job markets, it's essential that you commit yourself to life-long learning. Oh, I'm not saying that you have to go back to school and earn another degree (although it may make career sense to). What I'm saying is that the workplace is in constant motion—new techniques, concepts, and tools are introduced constantly. If you don't look forward, you will be left behind. It's your choice, so in effect, you choose the path that opens for you and your career.

Most businesses need to borrow funds at some time to either expand their operations or meet a financial crisis (such as when an account receivable doesn't pay its bill on time and normal business expenses need to be paid). A line of credit may be in order.

As with credit cards, too much of what seemed a good thing can get you in financial trouble. Before you borrow any money, know the true costs. Some loans spread their interest charges over the life of the loan; others charge interest upfront (car loans typically do this). This means that if you have a five-year loan and decide to pay it off early, say after three years, you will save little on interest. Why? Because the majority of the interest was front-ended—

charged in the early years and principal payment allocation was scheduled toward the end of the loan period.

Debt consolidation loans can reduce monthly debt payments. They can also lead to greater debt. How? By luring you into thinking that you have more money to spend. After all, you have less going out to pay the new loan than what you paid on all your other bills combined. You can buy more stuff! The only time it works is when you take your new found cash and pay down existing debt, as fast as possible.

Home values have increased significantly over the past decade. One of the hottest, and I mean hottest, areas to snag money from is the roof over your head. Equity. Open your eyes and ears to the ads—it's the "refi" siren beckoning to you.

Now, you could get that money and pay off any credit card debt—a good thing. But, and it's a big BUT, most people start charging again. Then they end up with a bigger loan against their home AND credit card balances. If you are going to use your built-up equity to pay off credit card debt, dump the majority of the credit cards and only use them for items you can pay off at the end of the month. Otherwise, the odds are against you.

 ***To Do:*** Identify loans (including credit cards) that you are currently repaying. Get your original loan documents and determine the number of payments, interest rate and how much you will pay in interest over the life of the loan. If you have misplaced them, call the lender and request copies.

- ✔ If you are buying your home, what is the interest rate? What is the original amount of the loan? Dig into your loan papers and find out what the balance of the home loan is with all the interest. Did you know that if you make one *real cost* extra house payment per year, applying it toward principal, that you can reduce a 30 year loan to 18 years?

  By paying bi-weekly (26 payments), you can reduce a 30-year loan to 15-years. You could save over $100,000 by paying every other week instead of once a month— an excellent addition to your retirement program!

- ✔ If you have outstanding student loans, find out what interest rates you are paying. In 1994, the Federal Direct Consolidation Loan program was introduced. It allows you to combine all federal student loans into one loan. The interest rate can vary, but it will never rise above 8.25%, according to current rules. For information, call 800- FED-AID (433-3243) or go to the website at *Mapping-Your-Future.org/paying/cnsldte.*

- ✔ For credit cards, two excellent websites are

*CreditCards.com* (Pros and cons of each will be disclosed, what the true costs are, how to qualify, etc.) and *CardRatings.com*. You can evaluate your credit cards against their competitors. It may make money sense to switch your balances to another company with lower interest charges—then start paying more down to reduce, then eliminate the outstanding balance.

✔ Get your credit cards out again—all of them (you can also use the most recent statement). This was recommended on Day 3 – Credit. If you were unsuccessful in getting the credit card company to reduce the interest rate charged, make another phone call and try again. Go back to Day 3 to get the script to use.

In retrospect, for each of your purchases, if you could roll the clock back, would you borrow the money for the same purpose again? Why or why not?

**Why:**

_____

_____

_____

_____

**Why Not:**

_____

_____

_____

_____


***Money $marts Tip.*** Your goal should be to be debt free, including what you owe on your home, by the time you retire.

# Part III
## Setting Up Your Safety Net

## (Days 12 – 17)

# 12     **Insure? . . . Maybe!**

*Most people need the assurance of insurance.*

**To Think About:** The only people for whom your life insurance will be useful are those you leave behind when you die. *If you have no dependents, you may not need any life insurance.* Life insurance is death protection. There are three basic reasons for buying life insurance:

**1**  To replace income if you die prematurely and others depend on you for income needs;

**2**  To provide immediate cash to pay debts, burial costs, and any estate taxes; or

**3**  To provide cash to buy out a business partner, repay business loans or hire a successor in case of an owner's death.

Insurance can be complicated and confusing. It doesn't have to be. Keep it simple and cost effective. In most cases, frugality wins. That means find the cheapest insurance with the most coverage and the best rating. How much coverage to carry is always a big question. Most insurance professionals and financial planners will recommend you carry six to seven times your annual income.

Who needs life insurance? Not everyone. If . . .

- You are single with no dependents—no, take a pass.
- You are single with dependents and not wealthy—yes, you need it.
- You are married with no kids—maybe. If your spouse or partner is self-sufficient and has the assets or income to meet financial obligations if you are gone, you don't.
- You are married with kids—yes. Unless, you are wealthy with lots of cash, you need plenty of insurance. Load up—now.
- You are married, don't work for pay yet have sufficient revenue sources and don't have dependent kids—probably no.
- You are married, don't work for pay yet have sufficient revenue sources and have young kids—probably yes. You need to determine the cost of child care and housekeeping services.
- You are retired—maybe. If your spouse will have

sufficient income from investments, retirement accounts and Social Security, you don't need it.

- You own a business—yes. Heirs may need it to pay estate taxes or partners to buy out your partner(s) heirs when the estate settles. If your heirs want to maintain the business, they could end up with business partners that may not be of their choosing—this gives them the money to buy your partner(s) out.

- You are rich—maybe. You may be wealthy, but if your assets are tied up in illiquid investments, you need cash to pay estate taxes.

- You are a kid—no. Unless you are a star or produce major money for your family, insurance is a waste of money. Wiser to put it in a type of investment account, like a mutual fund and instead, just buy more shares every time you would pay a premium.

## What's What in Insurance

There are two types of insurance and a zillion hybrids. *Term* and *Whole Life* are the most common. *Universal Life* was introduced several years ago, which combines the two—kind of—and then there are variations of each of these. You may come across Fixed or Flexible Premium, Fixed or Variable, One Insured or Multiple Insured, First to Die, Second to Die, even Blended policies.

All of them start from either a term or whole-life component. Anything outside of straight term or whole life will be a hybrid of the two. Some policies pay big commissions to agents, others very little.

*Term insurance* answers most needs when it comes to replacing lost income. The key parts of term are:

- You pay premiums every year (monthly, quarterly or annually). Insurance stays in force until you stop paying. There is no cash buildup/savings.
- With ordinary term, your premium increases slightly each year. You can buy a level term, which keeps the premium fixed for several years.
- Costs are determined by age, whether you smoke (if you haven't smoked for two years, you are considered weed free), and gender (although some insurance companies use unisex rates).
- Companies vary in what they charge—the same policy, and amount can cost twice as much at another company.
- It should be renewable—which means you don't have to re-qualify with a physical every year.

*Whole life insurance* has a savings account attached to it. The longer you are in it, the more savings you will have. In order to achieve this, whole life's premiums are much greater than term's.

When whole life is proposed, it is always accompanied by illustrations—the "what-ifs." Projections for growth in the savings side are *always* inflated—they are *never guaranteed*!

It's easy to be misled on interest rates. Insurance companies routinely announce high interest rates to keep policyholders happy; then they increase their operating expenses and charges for mortality (the death benefit). These expenses are deducted from your cash value before any interest is paid.

The result: you do get a higher interest rate, but it's paid on a smaller amount of cash. You, therefore, actually earn less than the promised rate.

*Universal Life* offers some flexibility. You can get a guaranteed policy amount for when you die; you can accumulate tax deferred cash; you can pay extra premiums early on so that extra cash will build up (theoretically), and your extra cash can pay future premiums. Here's the catch: if the interest or investment rates projected in your illustration are not achieved (after all, rates do vary) you may have a problem—your cash won't build up to pay the premiums down the road.

If you select one of the Universal Life-type policies, avoid the fixed interest option. Why?—many of these were sold when interest rates were higher, projections for accumulated interest haven't panned out. Over all, the stock market has out-performed the interest related markets for growth (meaning stocks have enjoyed a greater appreciation in value versus just receiving interest payments). The option you should look at is the *variable universal life* that is based on the fund's *mutual fund* performance. You will be able to compare apples to apples versus apples to who knows what.

## Disability

One type of insurance that is often overlooked is *disability*. It should be added to your insurance coverage as your cash flow allows. Your coverage should range from 50% to 70% of your present income needs and become effective 90 days after a disability. Why?—because policies are lower-cost and most people return to work within 21 days from either an accident or illness.

There are three general types of definitions that insurance companies use—

- Totally incapacitated and confined to bed
- Unable to work at any occupation
- Unable to work at a specific occupation

As in any contract, the small print can make it or break it. Here's what your policy should have:

- It should contain a *non-cancelable clause*. This means that as long as you keep paying the premiums,

the insurance company can't cancel you, no
matter what.

- It should have a *guaranteed annual premium clause,*
which means that premiums cannot increase that have
already been cited within the policy contract. As with
life insurance, the younger you are, the less the policy
will be.

- You want it to have a *waiver of premiums clause,* which
guarantees that if you do become disabled, you no
longer have to pay premiums to keep the policy in force.

- Ideally, your policy should have a *residual benefit
disability payment.* This means that if you are disabled
and eventually return to work at less pay than what
you received pre-disability, the insurance company will
pay the difference between what you used to get when
you were employed and what your new rate is.

- Finally, make sure that the wording in the policy states
that it will pay for any disability caused by illness as
well as by an accident.

## Long Term Care

What about LTC—long term care insurance? Your regular health
insurance coverage does not include long term care. None of
them do. An LTC policy covers the unexpected . . . the unexpected

that occurs when a stroke or a disability will require ongoing care. This is the care that most people do not want to talk about, much less think about. It's nursing care that is needed when you can't do it for yourself.

Nursing care is not cheap. A good facility will cost a minimum of $3,500 a month. That amount can gobble up savings and investments in no time.

I wouldn't be too worried about long term care until you hit your mid-50s. The cost will vary among insurance companies, so make sure that the quotes you get represent the same type of benefits. Below are a few of the areas that you should look for—

- The *benefit period* should be no less than four years, preferably lifetime.
- The *elimination period* refers to how long you have to wait before benefits start. Ideally, day one is when you want it to commence; the wait period should not be greater than 30 days.
- The *daily benefit* amounts refers to how much the policy will pay on a daily basis. Minimal is $100 for care in a facility and $50 within your own home care.
- An *inflation rider* stipulates how much the coverage will increase annually.

- A *home health care (HHC) clause* allows coverage at your home that is provided by approved health care providers. HHC differs from LTC in that long-term care individuals will most likely not return to their home.

Before you sign on the dotted line, it's important for you to know what the policyholder will need to do to qualify for the benefits. The three criteria are:

1. *Medical necessity* (i.e., your doctor says it's needed);
2. *Activities of daily living (ADLs).* This means that you are ambulatory, can bathe, dress and feed yourself, move about unattended, be continent and able to use the toilet; and
3. *Cognitive impairment* refers to not being able to think or act clearly. The most common references will be for dementia and Alzheimer's disease.

The insurance company you select should not be green in the selling of these policies. You want them to be in the business of LTC for at least 10 years and licensed in every state to do business, not just yours.

One source you can check out is AARP—American Association of Retired Persons (*AARP.org*). It makes sense that LTC is hot within this organization. They are constantly monitoring which insurance companies offer the best all around products.

*To Do:* Have an insurance check-up. Your policies can be evaluated by a Certified Financial Planner™ Professional who is paid by an hourly fee vs. commission (as in selling you another policy) or any insurance agent or broker who is a Chartered Life Underwriter. Tell them that you only want an evaluation now, not a pitch to replace anything.

Contact NICO, the National Insurance Consumer Organization at 121 N. Payne St., Alexandria VA 22314 or call 703-549-8050. NICO can tell you if the insurance company is having financial or consumer problems.

*To Do:* If your checkup indicates you are under-insured or wrongly insured, here's how to get low-cost insurance and keep your rates down:

- Don't smoke. Insurance companies consider you weed free if you haven't smoked in two years.

- Buy low-cost insurance. Contact a computerized price-quote service such as TermQuote—*TermQuote.com* or 800-444-8376, SelectQuote—*SelectQuote.com* or 800-963-8688 or InsuranceQuote—*InsuranceQuote.com*. Or go to the Internet, do a search on *Google.com* , *Clutsy.com* or *Yahoo.com* for low-cost insurance.

    You tell them your age, address, state of health, what kind and how much insurance you want. Basically, you are eliminating the commission that would have gone to a selling agent. No salesperson will call you.

- Buy annual, renewable term. In the majority of your key coverage years, it will be cheaper. There is no savings attached to it, just pure insurance. When you can, invest the difference that you save in premiums each year in a mutual fund.

- When buying any type of insurance, it's **Money \$mart** to be cautious. Make sure the company is Weiss rated ("A" ranking or better—call 800-289-9222 or go to the website, *WeissRatings.com*). There are five major insurance rating services: A.M. Best, Standard & Poor's, Moody's, Duff & Phelps, and Weiss Research. Weiss is the most conservative of the five—if Weiss doesn't give the company a good rating, take a pass.

***Money $marts Tip:*** Insurance is usually not a favorite dinnertime topic. So, don't use that format to do your planning. But do plan and implement your plan—anyone who is financially responsible for others needs to have adequate coverage.

# 13  Other Insurance

*Count your blessings if you
never have to collect on your insurance.*

**To Think About:** You will spend a lot of money on insurance, hoping that you will never need it. **Insurance is in your Money $marts life for all the "what-ifs."** You know you will die, someday. Life insurance protects those who are dependent on you. Disability insurance protects them, and you, if you are unable to work at what you normally do because of some unforeseen disability. Other insurance you will definitely encounter includes health, home and auto.

**Health insurance is obtained in case you or a family member has an illness, injury or accident that requires medical treatment.** As of this writing, health insurance and chaos seem to be in partnership. Health maintenance organizations (HMOs) are the most dominate provider for Americans today. An HMO requires that you use its approved doctors and hospitals.

That means you may have to switch physicians to have coverage. Some include dental and pharmacy needs for an extra fee.

Millions are without health insurance coverage. Seriously look at where your money is going. A critical illness or accident can wipe out your assets if you don't have coverage.

For some, it's a choice—as in, let's do great vacations and buy cars that have big monthly payments versus putting money into something that can't be seen or enjoyed.

For others, the job market could be the factor—you might be in-between. If that's the case, think short-term. Short-term policies are usually cheaper because they exclude existing medical conditions and pay less of your overall costs, but they are quite handy if something major hits. Two websites to know about—*eHealthInsurance.com* and *AssurantHealth.com*—both are leaders in this field.

**Automobile insurance is a must.** Most states require that you carry it. If you borrow money to finance the purchase of a car, the lender will require proof of coverage. Otherwise, it will purchase insurance for you and add it to your payment—a very costly hit on your checkbook.

**Homeowner and renter insurance cover a variety of areas**. For the owner, you want replacement contents insurance, as well as the standard fire, theft, and other types of possible damage coverage to the structure of your home. For the renter, your interest lies in contents and theft coverage. The landlord carries coverage (or should) for structural damage. Renter insurance costs less than homeowner insurance.

Think of any type of insurance as protection for you and your family if the worst happens. If you end up never making a claim on any of your insurance coverage, consider yourself unique . . . and blessed. If you do make claims, especially substantial ones, your money paid toward premiums may end up being pocket change. One major illness can financially cripple a family.

***To Do:*** Dig out all your policies and divide them into which kind they are. Identify what you pay annually, and in some cases, quarterly. Make a list with names, phone numbers and addresses of the agents and brokers who handle your insurance. *Place it in your file with all your other important documents and tell a family member or close friend where they are.*

When was the last time you had your policies reviewed and updated? Or, do you just automatically send in your money when the premium notices arrive without evaluating if you have the right kind or enough coverage? Either way, make an appointment with your agent to do an update. Be upfront and say that you are assessing your current coverage and not necessarily looking to purchase more.

At your appointment, if the agent shows up with scads of com-

puter generated data loaded with projections that may be unre-
alistic and not what you need, it's time to interview new agents.
The only projections that you should use are the ones *guaranteed*
within the policy, not "what-ifs." If you are considering switching
or adding to your coverage, get quotes from several different
insurance companies. The same coverage can be less, or more.

> Have an insurance checkup every two to three years—rates
> change, new products come on line.

**Money $marts Tip:** For all your insurance policies, cre-
ate a list that includes type of insurance, company, policy number, agent contact and phone number and the date you
made it. Every time you make a change to your insurance coverage—adding or deleting, it's a **Money $marts** move to update
the list. Give a copy to your accountant, attorney and immediate
family members.

To save premium money with insurance, do:
1. Shop around and compare premiums and terms with
   different companies (it's wise to use an agent that can
   represent several companies).

2. Increase your deductibles (instead of $100, increase to $500 or $1000)—do a spread sheet and compare how much you will save as you notch up the deductible.
3. To cover your "deductible" base, put aside the amount of your total deductibles in a savings account. This way, there are no surprises to your checkbook if you need to file an insurance claim.
4. Use your senior discounts (usually over 55)—insurance companies often reduce premiums charged to seniors.
5. Have your auto and homeowners with the same company.
6. Get a home security system.
7. Re-evaluate the value of your home—only insure the house, not the land.
8. Get healthy.
9. Delete coverage in areas when you don't need it (why pay for maternity if you've had a hysterectomy?).
10. Cease smoking.
11. Be loyal—some companies offer discounts to long-term policy holders (over five years).

# 14

# When There's a Will . . . There's a Way

*Anyone who cares plans for everything—
even the worst scenarios.*

**To Think About:** Most people die without putting in writing what they want done with their assets or how their families are to be cared for. They just assume that someone will step in and take care of things as they would want to be. Or, they assume that tomorrow is another day and that doing a Will can be deferred until there is more time to think about it. Life often doesn't run ideally and on schedule. Accidents happen. Terminal illnesses strike. People die before they are considered old. It's life.

If you don't make a plan for you or your family through a Will, your state will. You probably wouldn't like the results.

I came across an article several years ago, saved it, and now pass on a portion of it to you. It has been repeated numerous times in Ann Landers' syndicated column. It was written by Judge Sam Harrod III (retired), of Eureka, Illinois. Since I first discovered it, I tracked Judge Harrod down—he's become one of my e-mail pals and has graciously given permission to include this portion of the article in this book.

## The Statutory "Will" of John Doe

I, John Doe, make this my "will," by failing to have a will of my own choice prepared by my attorney.

1. I give one-half of all my property, both personal and real estate, to my CHILDREN, and the remaining one-half to my WIFE.
2. I appoint my WIFE as Guardian of my CHILDREN, if she survives me, but as a safeguard, I require that:
   a. my WIFE make written account every year to Probate Court, explaining how and why she spent money necessary for the proper care of our CHILDREN;
   b. my WIFE file a performance BOND, with sureties, to be approved by Probate Court, to guarantee she will properly handle our children's money;
   c. When our CHILDREN become adults, my WIFE must

file a complete, itemized, written account of everything she has done with our children's money;

d. when our SON and DAUGHTER become age 18,
they can do whatever they please with their share of
my estate;

e. no one, including my WIFE, shall have the right to
question how our CHILDREN spend their shares;

3. If my WIFE does not survive me, or dies while any of
our CHILDREN are minors, I do not nominate a
Guardian of our CHILDREN, but hope relatives and
friends may mutually agree on the one, and if they
cannot agree, the Probate Court can appoint any
Guardian it likes, including a stranger.

4. I do not appoint an Executor of my estate, and hope
the Probate Court appoints someone I would approve.

5. If my WIFE remarries, the next husband:
a. shall receive one-third of my WIFE'S property;

b. need not spend any of his share on our CHILDREN,
even if they need support; and

c. can give his share to anyone he chooses, without
giving a penny to our CHILDREN.

6. I do not care whether there are ways to lower my
death taxes, and know as much as possible will go to
the Government, instead of my WIFE and our

CHILDREN. In witness whereof, I have completely failed to make a different will of my own choice with the advice of my attorney, because I really do not care to go to all that bother, and I adopt this, by default, as my "Will."

*(no signature required)*

Sounds horrible, doesn't it? Without writing one, everyone has a "Will." The legal term is dying intestate—without a Will. If you don't choose one on your own, you get the one your state picks for you. Would you choose the one that Judge Harrod has shared? Most likely, no.

## You should have a Will to:

- Explain exactly what you want to do with your assets.
- Distribute any money or property received by your estate after your death (lawsuits and settlements occur after death).
- Reduce any death taxes.
- Name someone (the executor) who will shepherd the handling of your estate (not an easy task—you want someone who is organized, not scattered and has the time).
- Name someone to provide for your kids. Do not

assume that your brother or sister will welcome them with open arms for the rest of your kids' life. It's critical to discuss guardianship with the potential guardian. If your kids are elementary school age or older, tell them what you are thinking. They may have some strong thoughts about some of their relatives—who they would like to be with and who they would not want to be with.

- Guide and handle your children's inheritance.
- Avoid any problems that joint ownership can create.
- Even if you think your finances are in a mess or you have little in assets, having a Will eliminates confusion and uproar among your family.

***To Do:*** If you have not done a Will, do one before the week is out. So should your spouse or partner. If you have a Will, when was the last time you updated it? Any change in tax laws or personal circumstances demands a checkup. Before you see an attorney who specializes in Wills and Estates, take the time to write a holographic (do-it-yourself) Will that works for the short term until a formal document is drawn up. You can also purchase software specifically designed for creating your Will (*LegacyWriter.com, Nolo.com, MakeYourWill.com,* and *StandardLegal.net* are some of many programs available—prices range from $10 to $50). Make sure you sign it. It's recommended that you have the attorney do the final Will. You may think that you are clear in your instructions; a court may disagree.

## Change your Will when:
- You have children—either by birth, adoption or marriage.
- Your net worth increases, or decreases.
- Your child(ren) marries, separates or divorces.
- One of your heirs dies.
- You have a child who has an illness that may last indefinitely.
- There are any changes in the inheritance or property laws—federal or the state you live in.
- If you move or acquire property in a state that is not your residence.

***Money $marts Tip:*** The average working person spends over 10,000 days making money. Now's the time to do an inventory of what you have. Your question is—where do you want it to go when you die? Unfortunately, over 75% of those who will die today won't have a written will. Don't be in the majority—create a Will now.

# 15
# Planning a Comfortable Retirement

*Cushy beds take time to construct.*

**To Think About:** Fifty seems to be the magic age marker when you realize that the years for salting away money and investing for retirement have raced by. The younger you are, the lesser the amount you need to invest and save for your future years. The older you are, 50 plus, the more you must invest to get the same amount of income. Is it hopeless if you are just starting to pay attention at 55? No, just more work.

The primary goal of retirement savings and investing is to make your money last longer that you do.

The problem of not planning or having enough is twofold: most think that they are in fairly good financial shape and they are not (after all, I'm going to work forever so I don't need a lot of money!); and most do not save or invest enough of the monthly income. That, coupled with the fact that the average life expectancy is now in the mid-80s.

What about Social Security? Many refer to it as Social Insecurity. Over 90% of Americans under the age of 39 believe that they will never get back the amounts that they are paying in. They have a better chance to win a multi-state Power Ball Lottery!

Today, the average Social Security payment is slightly less than $800 per month. Living on Social Security alone means that you will be living below the federal poverty level. Presently, almost half our senior population is slated to do just that because of poor or no planning for their retirement years.

Because of the aging baby boomers, substantial amounts of funds will be required within the next 25 years. There's a strong probability that benefits and payments may be deferred or reduced to ebb the financial drain expected within Social Security and Medicare.

Will there be Social Security in the future? The answer is "yes," in some form. With the political winds changing, the question is, "What will it look like?" The best advice I can give you is to know what you are projected to get, review any changes in benefits annually (trust me, the media will shout them) and plan to build as much as you can independently.

Social Security is not going away, though some would like to eliminate it totally. It will have some tweaking. Use what you receive as a supplement, don't plan on it as the main course of your retirement portfolio. After all, it was never set up to be that in the first place.

**To Do:** Find out how much you have paid into Social Security and what other types of retirement accounts are available to you

- Call the Social Security Administration at 800-722-1213 and request the PEBES form—Personal Earnings and Benefits Statement. You can also request it online, *SSA.gov.* It will reflect your earnings and the amount you and your employer(s) have paid in. It will also project the amount of money you can expect to receive when you are eligible. If you find any errors (earnings or payments that haven't been credited), you have 39 months to notify Social Security.
- Are you presently contributing to a 401(k), an IRA, KEOGH, a tax-sheltered annuity program —403(b) or any other type of pension or profit sharing plan?
- If your employer offers a 401(k) or a 403(b), does it contribute to the retirement account on your behalf? Do you contribute the maximum amounts allowed? Do you have *choices* of where your money can be invested?

- Guesstimate what you will need in income for when you retire. A reasonable rule to use is to take 75% to 80% of your current expenses in all areas. It's assumed that you will spend less on consumer items, insurance and taxes. This can be further reduced by eliminating items that your family has declared "not needed."

> Our guesstimate of how much we need per year
> is _____ x .80 = _____

- Other than Social Security, guesstimate what your 401(k), 403(b), IRAs and other programs and investments will yield annually. Many offer projections with their annual statements. For guesstimating purposes with your other investments—stocks and mutual funds—take their present values, increase them in value 7% per year until retirement age. Now, calculate a withdrawal of 7% per year on the overall value of the investment for an annual yield.
- More guesstimating—the IRS has a variety of tables that will show you how much you have to withdraw from your various retirement plans at the year you

reach the age of 70½ (you must start to withdraw funds at this age)—check them out.

- When you receive your PEBES form back from Social Security, add that amount to your other estimates of income from investments and other programs you are in. Are you over, or under, your projected annual income needs?

---

If you are over, congratulations! If under, you need to re-evaluate your income resources and spending allocations. This is one area where procrastination—deferring until next month or year for a plan of action—doesn't work.

---

***Money $marts Tip:*** Do you need a million dollars or more in the bank when you retire? Probably not, unless you are really spending big money every month. Most people spend less post retirement. If the mortgage is paid off and you don't have to spend money on work related transportation, clothing, meals, and the like, or money for training and education, you may have reduced your monthly financial needs by several thousand dollars each month. What you need to do is crunch the numbers and make some realistic projections. It's all part of planning.

# Savings that Work

*Every dollar saved creates more.*

**To Think About:** When it comes to savings, most people just don't save enough money. It's approached with a "left-over" mentality. Maybe money is put in savings during the month, maybe not. On Day 9, you worked on your *Spending Plan*. In the section identified for "Fixed Expenses," Savings was included. Think of savings as a *tithe*—an amount that you allocate every month that is a percentage of your overall income.

One of the purposes of developing your *Spending Plan* was to identify areas where there was "fat"—money that anyone in your family fritters away, almost unconsciously. Those are the perfect funds to use to seed the beginning of your *tithe* to yourself.

> Pay yourself first. Your goal should be to save a minimum of 10% of your gross income each month.

## To Think About: A Liquidity Fund— Everyone Needs One!

A savings account should always be in a liquid format—this means that you can get your hands on it, all of it, within seven days. Ideally, your *Liquidity Fund* should contain anywhere from three to nine months of money needed to pay your ongoing expenses. Until you have this money set aside, do not buy or invest in items that are not needed.

"What's a Liquidity Fund?" you ask. It's not a backlog of water, coffee or soda. A Liquidity Fund is a critical ingredient in any household. Just as appropriate as insurance coverage, spending plans and paying your obligations.

It's money—the green stuff. It's your special stash when rainy days or bad news hits. Safe money that is readily available. *Money that you can access within seven days, with no strings attached.* Four questions surface: why, when, how much and where do you put it?

Let's start with the "why." Think of your Liquidity Fund as your personal, self-funded disability insurance policy. Think of your friends, family members, co-workers.

- Have any of them ever lost time from work because of illness, injury, sickness or the need to take care of personal business?

- Have any ever had a baby or needed to take care of a parent or sibling?
- How about you—have you ever felt that you needed to take a sabbatical?
- Has someone close to you, including yourself, lost a job or been downsized in salary?

A Liquidity Fund is there for financial assistance when you may be pulled away from activities that routinely create income.

"How much" should be squirreled away? There's a range. Comfortably, anywhere from three to nine months after tax income should be put aside. Here's something else to take into consideration. If the need arises, and you must withdraw and use your money, the amount of income you need per month will most likely be less than what you currently make.

Why?—because, if you are not earning a salary, your federal and state tax obligations will be less. You won't be paying into Social Security. Determine the exact amount of money you need each month to meet your regular obligations. Take that "needed" amount and multiply it three to nine times. This is the goal to accrue into your Liquidity Fund.

"Where" you put your money is important. These funds should be minimal to nil in risk. Use a money market fund, certificates of deposits and US Treasury Bills. Remember, the rule is to get your money—at least the original funds—out within seven days. And, although the money market account offered by your bank or savings and loan usually pays 1% to 1½% *less* than what the mutual fund companies offer, if you invested in a mutual fund or individual stocks, there is no guarantee that they will be worth a specific amount of money at any one time. This is the time to be safe.

The "when" is the easy part. Start it now. Today. A Liquidity Fund should be part of your operating budget—your spending plan. Before you commit to investing, salting money away for that special vacation or new car, this is the item you should concentrate on. You never know if misfortune or disaster will be on your life menu.

### *To Do:* Finding Money

One of the challenges is to find money to allocate for savings and investments. Here's some ways to add to the kitty—

- Do you go out to eat? Don't, or at least, reduce the number of times you frequent a restaurant— the fast food type or sit down with tablecloth. By the time you order a beverage, lunch or dinner and add the tip, you could have easily paid for the cost of a week's lunches that were toted from home.
- Bypass convenience foods. I know, they are so

convenient. But, that's the problem. Convenience costs money. Usually, at quite a premium. Forget about things you put in the microwave. Do they really taste that good?—most likely, not. They are just faster when you are in a hurry.

- Switch brands. Go generic. It's amazing how much more we pay for things that carry the brand names. A rule of thumb—the fancier the package the product is in, the less the actual item costs to produce. Brand X saves a lot of money.

- When's the last time you had a garage sale? This is a perfect family enterprise where everyone pitches in, cleans out his or her respective domain and hauls it all out to the family driveway. With a few well-placed signs on a sunny day, it's not uncommon to collect several hundred dollars for "stuff" that was just lying around.

Suggestion: what doesn't sell should be donated to a local charity. Do yourself a favor and don't haul it back in the house again. If you itemize your federal taxes, then Uncle Sam may help you save a few in tax dollars with the amount deducted.

One year, my family actually replaced a dying TV with a new improved and much bigger version by pooling all the proceeds from the garage sale. This had been agreed upon earlier by all. We even had money left over that went to the savings kitty.

***To Do:*** Determine how much three to nine months of your expenses are. If you don't already have investments with a mutual fund company (they all offer money market funds within their family of funds), open an account with a no-load fund (meaning that they don't charge you a commission).

Your local newspaper usually lists on a weekly basis what the top money market funds are paying. Note the names, look up their phone numbers and websites (*Google.com, Clutsy.com, Yahoo.com* and *CNN.com* all can connect you with money market funds). Note also what is the minimum each fund requires to open an account and what type of money instruments (US Treasuries, CDs, etc.) the fund purchases. Any stock brokerage firm, including discount firms such as Charles Schwab and Fidelity, offer their customers money market funds. Make a few phone calls and request a prospectus on their fund.

Most people think of income generated from money market funds as interest. The IRS calls them dividends and any money earned is reported as dividends. The amount you earn can change daily. It will be a factor of what the money instruments are yielding within the fund. You don't pay a commission, but it isn't free. An administrative fee is charged internally before your yield is calculated. So, if the fund is paying 2.25 %, it is a net amount— and it sure beats 1.25 % from the bank!

Your *Spending Plan* tracking should begin to show costly habits. Do you eat lunch out every day—do you need to? Do you smoke or drink? Brown-bagging it two days a week could yield $500 to $600 extra each year. Smoking and drinking can hit your wallet for thousands every year. Continue to probe on ways you can save . . . every dime counts.

***Money $marts Tip:*** The end result is this. If you want to cut back spending, most likely you can. If you want to save money, most likely you can. If you want to work, play and live within your cash flow, you can. The choice to do so is up to you, and your plan. And, wherever you place your money, make sure that you can access it—by check, phone or wire transfer.

# 17 Giving . . . What Goes Around, Comes Around

*To give is to get.*

**To Think About:** You don't need a PhD to know that there are people who are destitute. Destitution can mean that they are flat-out broke, even living on the streets, or that they have, or are suffering from, some horrible fate: terminal illnesses, horrendous accidents, home and building fires, theft or abandonment.

Mother Nature's deck of cards routinely deals hurricanes, typhoons, earthquakes, tornadoes, floods and forest fires. All guarantee incredible loss of property, injury and, sometimes, loss of life.

When you hear of someone's misfortune—another city, state or country, you probably think, "Thank God that hasn't happened to me, to us, here . . ." But what else do you do? Do you call and offer to help, send clothing and food, offer money or physical labor?

If faith is a factor in your life, do you practice your belief and support of it by actions and checkbook? Do you have a favorite organization that you have found yourself wishing you had more time to donate to?

> Charity is not a gene you are born with. Charity and giving are taught. You are the guide in your household.

 ***To Do:*** Create a support unit for a special cause.

- If you have kids, ask them if they know of any kids in their school who are undergoing any medical treatments—it's not unusual to learn that kids are getting chemotherapy or radiation, waiting for an organ transplant or some other procedure and still attending classes. Their families may be stretched to the limits and dependent on donations to continue treatments. Or, a week of meals, cleaning, or someone to just listen.
- Scout your local papers, radio and TV. Has any person or family undergone a devastating experience? What items, in good shape, aren't you using that could be

delivered? How about donating shelter and food for a few weeks?

- Contact a Gilda's Club, Ronald McDonald House or your local humane society. Is there a family or animal that needs some TLC or other type of help?
- Contact your church, synagogue or other religious organizations in your area. Ask if there is a family that needs your support—financially, emotionally, spiritually or all three.
- Adopt a grandparent. There are millions of senior citizens who are lonely and would cherish time with you and your family.
- Contact a homeless or battered women's shelter. Most have "wish lists" of items needed. See what's in your cupboards that you can donate. Your entire family can take on the responsibility to gather up several items by contacting your friends, neighbors and relatives for their support. For years, I've made it a practice to donate cases of books to shelters within my state.
- Develop a notebook to identify and track your good deeds.

These are just a few ideas to start with. Brainstorm different ideas with your family and see which ones fit your time, energy and money. When you give to someone else, you often become the biggest receiver of the gift you intended.

***Money $marts Tip:*** I have never met a person who has regretted helping someone in need. Helping doesn't always mean cash—time and just being present is a priceless gift.

# Part IV
## Family Talks

## (Days 18 – 20)

# 18    Credit Revisited

*Take credit for what is due,*
*but don't overdo what credit is given.*

**To Think About:** On Day 3, you contacted the three credit reporting agencies for copies of your credit report. By now, you should have received them.

How do they look? Any surprises—debts and accounts that you don't recognize or know are not yours? Were you aware that you had credit with as many creditors as reported or that you owed as much as the reports say you do?

The average rate paid on a credit card balance is over 18%. Collectively, Americans carry balances in excess of $953 billion on their cards—that's $150 billion-plus in interest! For every $9,200 in debt (the national average), $1,180 is added for interest charges. Credit card companies are routinely slapping an extra $20 to $39 charge on your balance if you are *one day* over the day due or you go *one dollar* over your pre-assigned limit. That could amount to a 100% plus interest charge! Ouch, ouch, ouch.

If you have negative information on your reports, it hangs around for not just months, it's years. Some states have legislated specific time periods that information is retained on your records—i.e., New York has limited it to five years. Most of the country uses the guidelines below:

| | |
|---|---|
| Bankruptcy | 10 years |
| Collections | 7 years |
| Default on Student Loans | 7 years |
| Late Payments | 7 years |
| Tax Liens | 7 years |

## Pay Attention to What You Are Being Dinged For

The interest charges and amounts charged by both credit card companies and banks are outrageous in most cases. Both play lop-sided, non-consumer friendly games with their "customers." They charge outlandish interest rates as well as late and over limit fees.

Be prepared to challenge and move your business. Your goal is to pay balances down, difficult when you are being hit for charges right and left. Tell them that you intend to tell everyone you know about their deceptive practices . . . than do it.

**Summing up**—it pays to pay your bills on time and keep credit card usage down. If this hasn't been your routine, start here— it's amazing how even one year of timely bill paying and the beginning erosion of outstanding credit card debt can improve your overall score.

***To Do:*** It's time to get your credit house in order, to seriously attack any outstanding balances that you continue to carry month-to-month. If there are any errors, you must take measures to correct them immediately; they don't get corrected by themselves. Most items—positive and negative—stay on your credit report for a minimum of seven years. A personal bankruptcy, 10 years. That's a heavy penance for credit misuse and/or bad times.

- Identify all errors—late reportings that weren't late, accounts, liens, collections that are not yours, etc. If an account has been paid off and it's not reported as such, say so. Anything you believe or know to be incorrect, challenge it in writing. If you have copies of correspondence that proves the debt or payment history is incorrect, enclose a copy with your challenge.

You can now send your protests in via the Internet as well as by regular mail.

- The bureau has 45 days to contact the reporting merchant or agency to verify its accuracy. If the merchant doesn't respond, their report must be removed from your file. You will be sent an updated copy of your report. *Don't expect the discrepancies to be corrected with your first challenge.* It may take months to finally sort it all out because creditors don't respond in a timely manner, the bureau fails to follow-up, or your challenge is ignored and the erroneous information is retained. Be diligent in your quest to ensure accuracy.

- Limit the number of cards you have and use. Today, you only need a general Visa and/or MasterCard and a business card, such as Diners Club or American Express.

- Resolve that you will only use your card for items that you can pay off within 30 days. If it's too tempting, stop using the cards. Stick them in your freezer or cut them up. Every extra dollar you get goes to paying off the balances.

- Ditto with your ATM card. It's too easy to withdraw cash and forget to enter the amount received in your check register. *Instead, get a debit card.* It looks like and feels like a regular Visa or MasterCard, yet it isn't. Each time you use it, your checking or savings account is debited. So, make sure you enter the amount into your check register.

---

Avoid all credit-repair "clinics" and "specialists" who promise to solve your credit problems. Don't give them one penny of your money. You begin to "fix" your credit by:

1   Paying all bills on time;
2   Reducing credit card and loan balances; and
3   Paying more than the minimum amount requested.

Pennies lead to dimes; dimes to dollars—don't pooh-pooh mini-amounts of money. This becomes "found" money and can add up to a tidy sum.

---

Stop your mailbox from filling up with more offers and solicitations. Most offers are "pre-approved"—credit card companies contact the credit bureaus (Experian, TransUnion, Equifax) and with their various formulas, determine who is "creditworthy." If you meet their criteria, the pitch is on the way.

Here's three things you can do quickly stop the credit pitch mail: (1) contact each of the credit bureaus in Day 3 and tell them you're not interested and to block companies from using your credit information; (2) call 888-567-8688 and instruct them to notify all three bureaus to block info from going out; or (3) go online at *OptOutPrescreen.com* to opt out for five years to indefinitely. You will need to give your name, Social Security number, date of birth, and address.

## Are you in credit trouble?

Do you only . . .

- Pay the minimums each month?
- Not pay on time?
- Avoid opening envelopes because you think it might be another bill?
- Not save a dime?
- Never pay cards off?
- Get turned down for credit?
- Hope the mail brings you another offer for another card?
- Routinely bounce or overdraft checks?
- "Forget" to sign a check so that you get a few extra days?

- Deny that there isn't enough money to your spouse or partner and yourself?

***If you answer "yes" to two or more of the above queries, get help—NOW.*** Contact the Consumer Credit Counseling Service at 800-388-2227. This 800# will refer you directly to the office closest to where you live. You can also go to the website, *CCCSintl.org* for additional information and articles.

## Wealth Building

A new and effective approach to eliminating your debt is an area called "Liability Management". A professional certified as a Financial Liability Manager will help you identify and organize your entire liability portfolio—including credit cards, personal loans, vehicle loans, student loans and mortgages. The manager will offer innovative solutions to better manage your debt that will, with mathematical precision, eliminate ***all*** creditor obligations, including mortgages, in 7 to 10 years.

This is excellent news, especially if you are in the 50-55 age range. Imagine—debt free by the standard retirement age! And, it could be much sooner the earlier you start in one of these programs.

Your monthly payments shouldn't increase and there should be no out-of-pocket expenses. One of the primary benefits, besides being debt free, is that your credit ratings will go to the top tier.

There are several companies that offer these services. As with anything financial, check them out and get references-people who have been working with them for years. The Internet is a great source to begin your exploration . . . make sure that you Google a company's name and add "scams" or "problems" to it as well . . . you never know what might pop up!

***Money $marts Tip:*** Credit is as common as water in the faucet. If the water gets rusty, you turn it off. If you are over-burdened with credit, you have to do the same.

# 19  Dark Clouds Can Surface

*Withheld news feels like bad news.*

**To Think About:** Even perfect families hit a few potholes along the way. We adults often attempt a classic cover-up—at all costs, keep bad news from the kids. Sometimes, even our spouse or partner. The reality is, family members have extrasensory perception . . . they can feel the dark cloud vibes in the air. No matter how you try to fake it, they know something is up, or wrong.

When bad news hits—a job loss or cutback, a death, accident or critical illness—it is normal to try and protect your loved ones from the news and its possible impact. Is it good to attempt to keep it from them? Probably not. They know you too well. They can sense your anxiety, fears and concerns. It's as if they can see and hear through walls and doors.

Years ago, I went through a devastating business loss. A partner had stolen several hundred thousand dollars from one of my accounts. Needless to say, it changed our lives.

At the time, my kids ranged from 12 to 16. I told them that things didn't look good and that there was a possibility that we could lose our home. They were also told that no matter what, I loved them and would make sure that there was some type of roof over our heads, that there would be food and heat and that they would have sufficient clothes to wear. The basics of life.

I promised to answer any questions that were asked. My family was told not to make demands—that I needed all the energy I could muster during this difficult time. In the end, we lost all material assets—our home, investments, even my business. We were broke.

Because I told my kids what was happening, there was support, even encouragement, from my closest rooting section. We were in it together—we were a team with a goal for survival and surviving together.

***To Do:*** If you are facing a sticky situation—a reduction in pay, potential layoff, money problems, or possibly someone you care for is critically ill or has been injured—call a family meeting. Your concern should not be, do you ***let*** your family (or friends) know how bad it is? Rather, it should be ***how*** do you let them know?

Tell them the truth to the degree that each can understand for his or her age. Do it sooner, rather that later. If your news involves a work or money problem, assure your family that you love them and will make sure that there will be ample food, heat, sufficient clothing and a warm bed to sleep in. If money is an issue, tell them everyone needs to cut back, no frills allowed. And, when it is over, if it is, call another family meeting and let them know you, and they, survived.

If it's something that hangs around, let them know you are hanging in there, give them a mini-update based on what their age can understand and absorb.

Now, it's your turn. Get out your pencil and identify problems and issues that may be creating a cloud over your household:

## What problem(s) do you need to talk with your family about?

_____

_____

_____

_____

_____

_____

## How did they react?

_____
_____
_____
_____
_____
_____

## How do you plan on letting them know what happens?

_____
_____
_____
_____
_____
_____

***Money $marts Tip:*** There is a difference between being wealthy and being rich. Wealth is all about money. Being rich is how you live your life. Even when money seems on the short side, you can be incredibly rich.

# 20 Keeping Holidays in Perspective

*Celebrations don't have to break your bank account.*

***To Think About:*** If you have kids, you know what the "gimmes" are. If you don't have kids, and have friends and relatives who do, or you've ever been in a store, you have witnessed the gimmes. It's a childhood disease that becomes epidemic when holidays and birthdays approach. And, no wonder. The media, through advertising, blitzes kids with every kind of conceivable toy and doo-dad. Kids have a hard time deciding what treasure they want. If the truth be told, they want them all. "Gimme this and gimme that!"

How about you? Do you get the adult gimmes? Do you go hog-wild during the holidays with gift *buying* for one and all? Do you *expect* gifts from all your friends and relatives?

Several weeks before I hit the big 50, I sent an email to all my friends and family and asked them not to spend any money on gifts for me. What I wanted instead was for them to support groups that needed money—my favorite was a program that their money would buy critters—be they chickens or cows—for families in Africa (*WomenInternational.com*). What fun it was to receive emails from the group saying that pigs, goats, even a cow were bought.

My friend John asked all his friends to forget his big 50 as a reason to give him a personal gift. A family in town had just had their home destroyed by a fire and had no insurance. He asked his friends to bring gifts, all wrapped, for the family to his birthday party. Many brought more than one. The greatest impact was on his teenagers. They loved the fact that Dad came up with this neat idea to help someone else and still enjoy his birthday.

Comedian George Carlin created a hilarious routine on "stuff." Most people have plenty of stuff; some have way too much stuff. Before adding to your closets, shelves and garages, do a reality check. Maybe someone else could use some of the stuff you already have.

***To Do:*** Call a family meeting before the pizzazz and excitement of holidays and birthdays hit. Tell them that you want to put together a spending plan for the next holiday season. Your spending plan could actually involve no money—time could be your currency.

- Everyone makes a list of potential gift recipients.
- Each family member decides what his or her money budget is.
- Determine what kind of gifts to be given: ideas include a store-bought present, homemade treats, time, money, even a donation in their name. Be open to possibilities that get generated from the "group think tank."
- Consider adopting a cause and tell friends and other family members that you don't want a gift given to you. Instead, tell them what or whom you would like a gift given to.
- Have each family member make a "wish" list. Family and friends can ask if there is anything specific someone wants. If budget and wishes fit, the days of returns will be eliminated.
- Large families routinely draw names and set a monetary limit to how much can be spent on a gift. Why not try it in yours to keep spending down?

Below is space for you to brainstorm other ways that your family can cut back spending, yet enjoy the special days and holidays. What can you come up with?

1. _____

2. _____

3. _____

4. _____

5. _____

***Money $marts Tip:*** It's not unusual to get something you really don't want. How about starting a tradition with family and friends with whom you exchange gifts and create Wish Lists? Kids that can't write yet can clip pictures from catalogs. That way, no one gets "junk" and everyone is sure to receive something that they really want.

# Part V
## Kids and Money

## (Days 21 – 23)

# 21

# Financing College Without Going Broke

*There's always a price for learning—*
*your bank account and experience.*

**To Think About:** When it comes to spending money on your kids and their education, college expenses win the prize. It will probably be the single biggest outlay of money you'll ever make over a four to five year period. Costs have increased, on average, a minimum of 7% per year for the last ten years.

If your kids are under 5, you could be looking at a tab of $250,000 for a four-year degree in the year 2010. A kid entering college within the next five years could tap your bank account for $75,000 to $250,000 or more. Ouch! What's a parent to do?

First, don't get spooked. Many programs are available to families at all income levels. The important thing to do is to start exploring. One of the first places to start asking questions is in the financial aid office of local schools—contact your community colleges, colleges and universities. Don't forget—private and public.

Why ask so many? Simple, you will most likely get different

answers. The more information you have, the more potential contacts.

In the mid-90s, the Gallup polls surveyed high school seniors. Over 25% were unaware of the availability of financial aid to help fund their education. It's their education, and it's totally appropriate for them to dig in and assist with the information gathering if they are old enough (14 years will do).

In 2001, I was the spokesperson for a company that surveyed several thousand parents. A huge percentage claimed that they would figure out how to pay for college when the day came to pay for it—that they just didn't want to deal with it now. That's pretty scary.

## Hidden Scholarships

There is free money out there—you just need to know where to look for it.

The Internet will be the quickest resource for you. Start with the following websites: College Board (*CollegeBoard.com*), FastWeb (*FastWeb.com*), Sallie Mae (*CollegeAnswer.com*) and Scholarship Research Network Express (*SRNExpress.com*).

Before you start your probe, do a little homework. Such as— why is your child unique—compile academic and outside school achievements. The purpose is to "shine." FastWeb lists over 600,000 scholarships—for everything from being short or over-weight to hobbies and hometowns.

Don't forget your employer or companies/stores within your community. Many have programs that support the locals, including Target and Kohl's.

 ***To Do:*** Here are a few ideas to get you started:

- If you have kids who are within two years of starting college, get to know the financial aid rules.
- Get a Free Application for Federal Student Aid by calling 800-433-3243 or through the website, *FAFSA.ed.gov.* Read it carefully so you don't short-change yourself. An example would be if you listed your retirement programs—IRAs, 401(k)s, 403(b)s and the like in the Assets section of the application. These items are NOT to be included. If you do, you could knock yourself out of the running.
- Apply for every form of financial aid you hear about and include all other rejection letters with applications. Colleges sometimes withhold offering aid if they think you haven't "tried" hard enough in seeking other sources.

- Send in applications early. The better grants and jobs are given out early. Grants are a good thing—they don't have to be repaid.
- Pell grants are a common source. At this writing there is a cap of $4,050 per qualifying student each year. Congress is looking at making adjustments in this area. Your best source would be your financial aid office to get the latest updates.
- Negotiate. If the school wants your son or daughter, they may be willing to sweeten their financial aid package. You don't get it unless you ask.
- If money is tight, start at the local community college. A transfer to a four-year school can be done at the junior year. The degree doesn't say how many years your child attended the institution—it just denotes the degree earned at graduation.
- Ask if there is a tuition break if more than one family member attends the same school.
- Ask your alma mater if it offers reduced rates for alumni's kids.
- Ask your bank if it participates in the CollegeSure CD, a special CD that pays a floating rate of interest that is tied to the cost increases of the 500 colleges in the Independent College 500 Index. For information on the

CD, call the College Savings Bank at 800-888-2723 or go to the website, *CollegeSavings.com.*

- Set up investment and savings accounts for each kid under UTMA—the Unified Transfer to Minors Act. UTMA allows you to control money until your kids are 21 versus UGMA (Uniform Gifts to Minors Act) which stops at 18.

- Every state has a 529 Plan. Parents, grandparents, other relatives and friends can put money in the fund for the purpose of paying for education—including books and board. There are no income limitations on eligibility and you control it. No taxes are paid on earnings that are used for educational purposes. If a scholarship comes into play, any unused money can be withdrawn without penalties (you do have to pay some tax here). If the child doesn't use it—money can be directed to a sibling. Most states have no limit for when money has to be used. At this writing, an account can be seeded with over $250,000.

- Start now and contribute regularly to an investment account for each kid. Reinvest all dividends and gains. Many mutual funds allow minimal investments of $25 to $50 if done on a monthly basis.

***Money $marts Tip:*** Do yourself, your kids and your money a favor by first investing in no-load mutual funds in their early years on a regular basis. As the teen years approach, make them your partner. Working during vacations and the summer months is a reasonable expectation in adding money to *their* college fund.

## 22

# Savings, Spending, Sharing and Allowances

*If they don't work, they don't get paid.*

**To Think About:** When my kids were young, on any Sunday morning, you would find my living room cluttered with the morning's papers laid out on the floor. The morning news shows were on in the background. Small hands were busy at work. With just a pair of scissors, dollars—lots of dollars— were being saved.

The Sunday papers are fantastic sources for coupons worth plenty. Why not show your kids how they can save money on essentials—the needs of the household—and get money back? Not a bad habit to start early in life.

**To Do:** From the ages of 6 to 10, you can have a tremendous impact on your kids' (or grandkids) **Money $marts**. These years are at the peak when it comes to accepting your guidance and influence. This is an excellent time to introduce comparison shopping and pricing.

- Show them what unit pricing is all about—your source will be the labels attached underneath the item on the grocery store shelf. Have them point out items pitched on TV and see if there is a similar item that is stocked. Compare prices and packaging.

- Scout your cupboards. Don't forget the bathroom— yours and the kids. What are the necessities? What items are always in stock (think shampoo, toothpaste, soap, cereal)? What items are occasionally purchased (think sweets or something needed in a favored recipe)?

    This age group is prime for learning about the differences between brands, cost, size, quality and quantity. Most like to read and look at pictures. Let them do it for you.

- Work with them on the differences of "do we need this" vs. "do we want this." With list complete, it's time to get out the scissors and ad pages. Your local paper probably does a great job in putting together the weekly specials. Coupon ads are wonderful. They usually include the exact packaging image of the item on them. If you live in an area that has competing stores, your kids can compare the "deals" at each.

Here's a hint. If your youngster has spied a coupon for his favorite cookie—Oreos—encourage him to clip it. It may not be on the "need" list—it's on the "want" list. That's OK. When you are ready to spring for a treat or reward, the Oreo coupon wins. It ends up being a reward—for you, you save some money,and for your son, he gets a goodie.

In the meantime, store the Oreo coupon in the "C" pile—an envelope—or slot in an expandable mini file that works well for coupon holding. "C" as in cookie. Much easier to track down. It makes more tracking sense to place your coupons in item or type categories instead of brand names.

Kids make great interns. As your assistants, show them where the directories for items are in the store. Point them in the direction of their coupon necessities. Encourage them to stay within their lists and keep track of how much money they are saving. Offer a prize for finding all their items.

Coupons are everywhere. Your newspaper, magazines, flyers left on doorknobs and windshields. Teach your kids how to take advantage of them. A few cents here, a few cents there, creates **Money $marts.**

### To Think About: To Allowance or Not to Allowance
One of the hot potatoes in family money is whether to give kids allowances. Contrary to popular belief, when kids get

one, it doesn't make them spend more money. If anything, they become more tuned into what they are spending and saving. Some believe that allowances should be earned and tied to specific jobs; others believe that they be given with few strings attached.

I think that allowances are good ideas, but given with restrictions. As in, if you don't do your regular jobs (feeding pets, making bed, etc.), you don't get one. After all, if you show up at your work, yet do little if any work, how long will it take you to get a pink slip? Why should a kid be any different? If they don't do their family jobs, why should they get paid? Allowances should be earned, not just handed over because it is Saturday.

> An allowance is money that a kid receives on a regular basis (usually weekly) as a payment for being a participating and working member of your family. No participation, no pay.

Allowances allow both you and your kids to talk money—how they spend, save, give and earn it. They aren't a cure-all for teaching about the use and misuse of money, but they do offer a giant step. The key question usually is: how much? Some parents pay per job and degree of difficulty; some, a specific amount every week; and some pay based on age.

The formula I settled on was based on age. I paid $1 per week per the number of years old. A 10-year-old gets $10 per week. You may be thinking, "Wait a minute—that's $40 per month, a lot of money for a 10-year-old." Yes, it is. But as parents, we get to attach strings.

*Here's what my allowance formula was when my kids were under my roof: 10% of all money received must be given to charity and/or church; the remaining amount is divided equally between savings and spending.*

My 10-year-old gave $1 to charity and church; put $4.50 into savings (every time there is $10, a deposit is made at the adult bank); and got to spend $4.50. How it's spent was decided by him (yes, I did have limitations here too). If he wanted pizza and it was not in my game plan, guess who paid? A soda, action figure or some other event? He paid. Those items become part of his spending plan, a mini version of what you have. Where did he keep his money? In three big, clear plastic jars, each with a label on it—*Spending, Savings* and *Sharing.*

Kids learn very quickly that once the money is gone, it's GONE! That's why the jars work; it's visually obvious when the money is gone. No more bucks (with some exceptions—very few) until the next pay day. You, as the Bank of Mom and Dad, need to set rules up ahead of time—such as, you are not open 24 hours a day.

You will discover that surprisingly, kids actually start spending less of your money when they must be accountable and responsible for their allowance allocations! And, they know that you can't be hit up for more money when theirs is gone.

If your kids are over the age of 3 and they know the difference between a dime and a quarter, have expressed the desire to buy something, know that money must be exchanged in order to get items from the store, or have displayed a gimme attack, you are ripe for introducing an allowance.

***To Do:*** It's time to get the kids involved—even if they can't read or write yet, they're players. You'll be working with them, so the young ones can point at things and you can scribe for them.

- Have your kids make their own personalized Spending Plan. Ask them to identify what they spend the money on that you give them or that they receive as gifts. And ask them to identify which items are "needs" and which are "wants." A small notebook is good for tracking expenses. Don't forget the computer. Kids are pros and can create tables to fill in. If old enough, they may want to try one of the financial software programs like Quicken or Microsoft Money.

- Tell your kids that you are going to shift how you dole out money to them. From now on, it's once a week.

- Decide which extra items you will be responsible for. It's a given that you will supply food, shelter and clothing. What if your daughter wants a designer pair of jeans, jeans that you don't consider necessary? Your answer should be, "She can save for them out of her spending funds."

- With your kids' input, decide how much will be considered "forced" savings, savings that can be used for bigger items, how much will be allocated toward a favorite charity and/or church, and how much they get to spend on personal items.

- If your kids have a special project or item that costs a year's worth of savings, consider a matching grant proposal—they raise half, you match it.

- Plan on revisiting their Spending Plans in 3 months to see how they are doing.

- Encourage them. Having **Money $marts** is a key growing up ingredient.

 ***To Do:*** Create Spending Plans for your kids. Next is one that we used for my Grandson Frank:

# Frank's Spending Plan

**Month** _____ **Week** _____

| Money Received | Mon | Tues | Wed | Thur | Fri | Sat | Sun |
|---|---|---|---|---|---|---|---|
| Allowance | ___ | ___ | ___ | ___ | ___ | ___ | ___ |
| Gifts | ___ | ___ | ___ | ___ | ___ | ___ | ___ |
| Odd Jobs | ___ | ___ | ___ | ___ | ___ | ___ | ___ |
| Other | ___ | ___ | ___ | ___ | ___ | ___ | ___ |
| TOTAL | ___ | ___ | ___ | ___ | ___ | ___ | ___ |

| Money Spent | Mon | Tues | Wed | Thur | Fri | Sat | Sun |
|---|---|---|---|---|---|---|---|
| Art Lessons | ___ | ___ | ___ | ___ | ___ | ___ | ___ |
| Camps | ___ | ___ | ___ | ___ | ___ | ___ | ___ |
| Candy | ___ | ___ | ___ | ___ | ___ | ___ | ___ |
| CDs | ___ | ___ | ___ | ___ | ___ | ___ | ___ |
| Cell Phone | ___ | ___ | ___ | ___ | ___ | ___ | ___ |
| Charity/Sharing | ___ | ___ | ___ | ___ | ___ | ___ | ___ |
| Church | ___ | ___ | ___ | ___ | ___ | ___ | ___ |
| Clothes | ___ | ___ | ___ | ___ | ___ | ___ | ___ |
| Computer Games | ___ | ___ | ___ | ___ | ___ | ___ | ___ |
| Crafts | ___ | ___ | ___ | ___ | ___ | ___ | ___ |
| DVDs/Videos | ___ | ___ | ___ | ___ | ___ | ___ | ___ |
| Gave to Friends | ___ | ___ | ___ | ___ | ___ | ___ | ___ |

# Frank's Spending Plan

**Month** _____ **Week** _____

| Money Spent | Mon | Tues | Wed | Thur | Fri | Sat | Sun |
|---|---|---|---|---|---|---|---|
| Gifts | ___ | ___ | ___ | ___ | ___ | ___ | ___ |
| Internet | ___ | ___ | ___ | ___ | ___ | ___ | ___ |
| Lunch Money | ___ | ___ | ___ | ___ | ___ | ___ | ___ |
| Movies | ___ | ___ | ___ | ___ | ___ | ___ | ___ |
| Parties | ___ | ___ | ___ | ___ | ___ | ___ | ___ |
| Pets | ___ | ___ | ___ | ___ | ___ | ___ | ___ |
| Savings | ___ | ___ | ___ | ___ | ___ | ___ | ___ |
| School Events | ___ | ___ | ___ | ___ | ___ | ___ | ___ |
| Snacks | ___ | ___ | ___ | ___ | ___ | ___ | ___ |
| Sports | ___ | ___ | ___ | ___ | ___ | ___ | ___ |
| Other | ___ | ___ | ___ | ___ | ___ | ___ | ___ |
| **TOTAL** | ___ | ___ | ___ | ___ | ___ | ___ | ___ |

**Total Money Received** $ _____

**Total Money Spent** $ _____

**Over / Under** $ _____

This is first step in establishing a lifelong habit of planned spending as well as dealing with expected income. It's a simple spending plan, but you can expand or contract it to meet your child's needs. Just make sure that you take into account that, like adults, children have fixed and variable expenses and income.

By the time your kids hit 6 years of age, their allowance should include the provision for some "walking around" money that can be spent on whatever they desire. As your kids approach the age of 10, the ability to match income with expenses should become evident. Your son or daughter should have a good grasp of the sources of his or her income and outgo.

Your 10-year-old should understand what expenses are fixed — such as school lunches and supplies—and a grasp of amounts to put toward savings and donations to charities and the church should also be evident. Your shining hour as their top role model is here. Kids at this age are very tuned in to how you save money — do you need to start saving now for next summer's vacation? And, how you spend it — ongoing family expenses.

The key here is to give your kids a road map to planning their spending plan. Discuss your family's spending plan: the how and why of the income and outgo, the successes and the failures in keeping to the spending plan. A monthly family spending plan session is an excellent tool to use for regular reinforcement of the concepts you are teaching your kids.

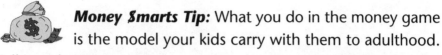 ***Money $marts Tip:*** What you do in the money game is the model your kids carry with them to adulthood. Talking about money is important; encouraging them to be discriminating about what they spend their money on is important; and as they mature, sharing with them some of your money mistakes is also important—we all make mistakes. Positive learning can come from those mistakes—don't bury them.

# 23  The Teen Challenge

*Teens and money go hand-in-hand. It's from your wallet-to-their-wallet that you want to control.*

**To Think About:** Teens are one of life's challenges. Most teens want to test their parents on just about everything. Maybe it's in their job description. When it comes to money, this group is a mighty force, spending over $100 billion a year! No wonder advertising and PR firms spend mega millions to entice your kids to their products.

You do your kids, and yourself no favors when you hand money over at their asking. It's not uncommon for families to talk about the perils of not telling the truth, stealing, drugs and sex. Yet, the majority are quite reluctant to talk about money. It's almost taboo, something that just isn't proper to talk about. These teens learn early about the Bank of Mom and Dad—one that has unlimited hours. For some, unlimited funds.

At some point, teens start pressuring for a car. Of course, they promise they will pay for it and drive ultra safe. The odds are that if your teen is a son, he will have an accident. Much lower odds for daughters—that's why car insurance for males under 25 years of age is so expensive. Where does the money come from?—usually an after-school job.

With a job, the odds now are that school grades will decline, alcohol and drug use begin or increase, materialism rears its head (if it hasn't already), and parental authority begins to vaporize. With that said, let's look at the pluses. After-school jobs help teens to mature and prepare them for the outside world. There is usually a sense of pride and an increase in self-esteem and confidence. Good things to have in the backpack of life.

> Your teen is not perfect. Teens make mistakes, lots of them. When they do, view it as an opportunity to discuss behavior and consequences.

Collectively, teens earn billions of dollars every year. The question is, do they also save billions? Nope. They outspend what they make by approximately $5 billion a year. Where does the excess come from—you get three guesses, only the first one counts— you, the Parent!

You can't help but wonder if a monster hasn't been created. What correlation can be expected between teens' spending and saving behaviors and those they display in adulthood, if they now outspend what they make by more than 5½%? The potential for indebtedness could be a financial back-breaker. It is, therefore, critical that your teen has broadly based financial management skills.

**To Do:** To find out what your teen knows about money management, duplicate the test below and have them take it. But first, take the test yourself, giving the responses you think they are likely to give. You will have some idea about the degree of penetration your money counseling has had in their minds. Better yet, your goal is that they will know the information in the quiz below by the time they get ready to leave the nest. Then, compare your teen's answers with yours.

## Teen Money $marts Quiz

1. Do you know how to open a checking account?                                    Yes ____ No ____
2. Do you know how to balance a checkbook?        Yes ____ No ____
3. Do you know how to open a savings account?    Yes ____ No ____
4. Can you name three types of savings programs, other than a passbook savings account?              Yes ____ No ____

5. Would you know how to stop payment on a
   check if you needed to?                               Yes ____ No ____

6. Do your outside earnings account for more
   than 15% of the total balance in your savings
   account?                                              Yes ____ No ____

7. When you run out of checks, do you know
   how to order more of them?                            Yes ____ No ____

8. Do you understand all the entries on monthly
   bank statements for both checking and savings
   accounts?                                             Yes ____ No ____

9. Do you know the difference between a bank, a
   savings and loan institution, and a credit union?    Yes ____ No ____

10. Do you know what interest rate is charged on
    the unpaid balance of your credit card or on
    one of your parent's credit cards?                   Yes ____ No ____

11. Have you been saving 10% to 25% of all
    money that you receive from parents, gifts
    and outside jobs?                                    Yes ____ No ____

12. Do you have money left over at the end of
    your pay period, either weekly or monthly,
    after all your expenses have been paid?              Yes ____ No ____

13. Do you know who to call if you lose a
    check book or a credit card?                         Yes ____ No ____

14. Do you know how to use an ATM card?                  Yes ____ No ____

15. Do you know how to get cash in an
    emergency — day, night or out of town?        Yes ____ No ____

16. Could you make up a livable spending plan
    for yourself without your parents' assistance?   Yes ____ No ____

17. Do you understand how to read a simple
    contract, such as the one found on the back
    of a credit card application?                  Yes ____ No ____

18. Do you know how to get car insurance?          Yes ____ No ____

19. Do you know what penalty or penalties are
    assessed when you make a late payment on a
    credit card?                                   Yes ____ No ____

20. Do you know what a credit report is and how
    to get a copy of yours?                        Yes ____ No ____

21. Savings accounts earn interest; do checking
    accounts?                                      Yes ____ No ____

22. Do you buy on impulse?                         Yes ____ No ____

23. Do you know how and when to file federal
    and state tax returns?                         Yes ____ No ____

24. Do you know what an IRA is?                     Yes ____ No ____

25. Do you know what travelers checks are and
    how to get them?                               Yes ____ No ____

26. Do you know what a lease is and what the
    contract should contain?                       Yes ____ No ____

| **How To Score:** | Give every *Yes* answer 2 points. Give *No* answers 0 points |
|---|---|
| **If your teen scores:** | |
| **40 to 52 points —** | Help him pack his bag, he's ready to leave home or perhaps even support you. |
| **25 to 39 points —** | He's on his way, but still needs input from you. He can read this book, so get him his own copy. |
| **24 and below —** | You both need to wake up fast, otherwise he will never be ready to leave home. You may have to support him the rest of your life. Not a good idea. |

***To Do:*** Ask your teen(s) if he wants to learn more about and how to use money and be a player in the adult world. It will be a rare teen who turns you down.

• If your teen has a driver's license, "hire" him or her as your personal assistant for a long vacation period, summer is ideal. This means that you are accompanied on various shopping expeditions and errands—groceries, cleaners, dropping off and picking up younger siblings, the vets, the bank—wherever you need to drive to and/or write a check.

Not only can your teen chauffeur you, he will pay for

everything you normally do by writing your checks and paying your bills. This includes mortgages or rent, taxes, insurance and the like. You get to sign the checks. Initially, he will think this is fun. After a while, it becomes a drag. Reasonable wage is the minimum federal wage rate. If it's higher in your state, then match it.

- Let your teens know how much money it takes to run your household. Open up your check register or the money software program you use on your computer. Have him make the entries for checks written and items that get automatically withdrawn from your account. If your income varies monthly, this is a perfect opportunity to discuss why you need savings backup and a realistic Spending Plan.

  When I did this with my teens, they were stunned at the amount of money it took to run our household.

- Check out "Hot" career projections in national magazines such as *Business Week* and *U.S. News & World Report*. The Internet is a great resource to see what is topical—the home pages of AOL, Yahoo, CNN, etc. commonly run workplace and career related articles.

- Your kids are on the Internet all the time—have them do a Google search for opportunities and print out the results. Ask your teen what kind of work sounds interesting. Discuss what various jobs pay and what kind of education or training is required.

- If your teen is car bound, set some rules up. Include financial and safety responsibilities. If your teen doesn't hold up her or his end of the bargain, privileges are suspended. Set up the conditions for any suspension and reinstatement of privileges when the driving license is first obtained.
- If your teen gets an after-school job, set up rules to monitor behavior and grades. Any violations, a family talk is in order. Set up a probation time-off. If grades or attitude don't improve, the consequence is that the job is terminated.
- If, and when, your teen gets a job for pay, make a condition that a percentage is set aside for savings. If money flows through fingers like water, offer to be the "bank" and withhold an agreed upon amount.

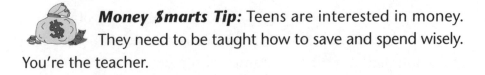 ***Money $marts Tip:*** Teens are interested in money. They need to be taught how to save and spend wisely. You're the teacher.

# Part VI
## Investing Savvy

## (Days 24 – 27)

# 24

# Your Shelter:
# Buying vs. Renting

*A roof of your choice creates roots.*

**To Think About:** Housing costs money, lots of it. If you decide to buy a home, it will be one of the biggest investments you make in your lifetime. One of your first steps will be to determine how much you can realistically afford to spend on your housing needs. Your accountant, a financial planner or an experienced Realtor® can assist you in the calculations.

As your family grows, your first home may no longer fit. It's too small. Or, as your kids move out, your housing needs may shrink. It's too big. Or, you like what you have, but you have decided to reduce your financial overhead by getting a smaller, less expensive place with little or no mortgage.

*Owning a home has tax advantages over renting.* Mortgage interest and any real estate taxes paid can be included in your itemized deductions when you file your income taxes. Other arguments for home ownership include equity buildup. This happens when you pay the mortgage down and/or the home appreciates in value. Equity is the difference between the amount your home is worth and your present mortgage balance.

Eventually, after years of paying your mortgage, your home is paid-off—a terrific strategy for retirees. The only housing expenses are real estate taxes, maintenance and repair.

> If you presently have a 30-year mortgage, you can shave 12 years of payments by making one extra payment per year. An extra $1,000 payment will create a nest egg of $144,000 in savings! That's an excellent nest egg to have.

There are circumstances where it makes **Money $marts** to rent your home instead of buy. Included are:

- Living in a rent-controlled area where you are already paying low rent;
- You are uncertain of your future for the next year or two;
- You are newly divorced or widowed;
- It looks like you have a job change within the next two years;
- Real estate values are decreasing;

- You don't have any savings for the down payment (there are mortgages that finance 100 percent, but make sure you read the small print if this becomes your chosen option).

***To Do:*** At some point, you will think about buying a home or getting a bigger home than the one you currently own. A home can be a house, condo, townhouse, mobile home, houseboat or a co-op. Before you do:

- Brainstorm with your spouse or partner, what you both want in an ideal home. What should it look and feel like? If your kids are school age, include them in the process. Think about location, recreation facilities, size, number of rooms, backyard needs, style and distance from work and school.
- If you buy a home (or presently own one), determine how much your personal federal taxes will be reduced per year because you can declare mortgage interest and real estate taxes as an itemized deduction.
- If you own a home and have the "we need something different bug," visit the model homes of a nearby development. Note what features you like, then get an estimate of what fixing up your present home yourself

would cost. Would you save any money by improving or remodeling your present home instead of buying a new one?

- Remodeling centers, such as Home Depot and Lowe's, give classes throughout the week on just about every imaginable project you can think of . . . and some you hadn't. Check out the schedule and enroll in one if you want to try your hand in the fix-up mode.

- In the area you live, or one you are considering buying in, what has been the average appreciation in value of the price range you are considering?

- If you currently rent, what are the advantages of buy-ing a home?

_____

_____

_____

_____

- If you currently rent, what are the disadvantages of buying a home?

_____

_____

_____

_____

Caution Alert: If one of your goals is to buy a home, make sure that you have done everything in the two chapters on Credit (Day 3 and Day 18). You want to know what your FICO score is and, if there were errors on your report, you need to begin the mending process ASAP.

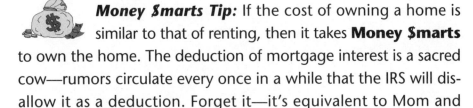 ***Money $marts Tip:*** If the cost of owning a home is similar to that of renting, then it takes **Money $marts** to own the home. The deduction of mortgage interest is a sacred cow—rumors circulate every once in a while that the IRS will disallow it as a deduction. Forget it—it's equivalent to Mom and apple pie—it isn't going to happen.

Warning: don't buy the biggest or best house in the neighborhood. The **Money $mart** buyer looks for the smallest house that they can live in in the best neighborhood. If it's a fixer-upper, even better.

# 25 Investing ABCs

*Investing is like gardening—*
*plant seeds, water, cut blooms and remove weeds.*

*To Think About:* The media routinely profiles someone who has evolved with a rags-to-riches story. Sometimes, there will be a story of how a woman who spent her life cleaning houses donated a million dollars to the local college. It happens. The question becomes, how could she do it when she only makes a few dollars per hour, and in some cases, per day?

The answer is fairly simple. She saved a portion of her money and invested it over a period of time. Her investments were in companies and products she understood and could get information on. That's the secret! Nothing ground breaking or earth shattering.

| Pigs get fat. Hogs get slaughtered! |
| --- |

As you start on your investing path, here are a few rules for your journey:

- *Never put all your money in one thing*—this means you don't invest all of your money in just one stock, one mutual fund, one piece of real estate, one bond, one business, etc. Diversify, diversify, diversify.

- *Invest (as in savings) on a regular basis.* By investing regularly, you will never pay top, or bottom, dollar for anything. It averages out.

- *Know what your financial and emotion tolerance for risk is.* If reaching your goal allows you several years of investing, you can usually undertake more risk. If your goals are short term or you need money within a few years, your risk level should be low. A **Money $marts** rule is that the higher the potential return, the greater the degree of risk; the lower the potential return, the less risk.

- *Do your homework.* Don't invest money because your friend is. The best investments are companies that make products that you know of, use and/or understand. Sometimes, weird things do very well. Sometimes they don't.

- *Select investments you understand.* Can you explain it to others (how about yourself)? Can you sleep at night? Invest in areas, concepts, and products that you understand. There's lots of choices out there—why go with something that feels alien?

- *Don't panic when bad news hits.* If you invest in the stock market, there are days, weeks, months, even years that your holdings may not appreciate much, or could depreciate in value. Over all, though, the stock market has outperformed other investments for the long haul.

- *Set specific goals, both on the upside and on the downside.* When you hit your objective, re-evaluate. Would you buy more of it at the current price? If not, sell at least half and reinvest your profits somewhere else.

   Always set a *floor* to how low you will tolerate an investment declining to. If it drops below your floor price, sell it. Too many investors hold onto their investments, hoping (and praying) they will eventually climb back to the price it was originally purchased at. Take your loss and move on. This is a *must do* strategy.

- *Once bought, don't ignore your holdings.* Investments, as in your *Spending Plan*, goal setting, insurance requirements and taxes, need to be looked at periodically. Don't stick them in the drawer and forget you have them. Think garden—your plants have to be watered,

pruned and weeded. At the minimal, annual reviews
are in order.

- *Trust yourself.* You have the smarts and savvy to make
decisions about  investments. Annually, a staffer at *The
Wall Street Journal* throws darts at the stock quotation
pages. The dart selections are then compared at year-
end with the selections of a panel of experts. More
times than not, the darts win out. So can you!

- *Averaging puts you ahead.* Dollar cost averaging (DCA)
is the process of making a regular investment in a stock
or mutual fund of a fixed amount of money at a specific or regular time.

    When you buy mutual funds, it is common to con-
tinue to put more money in the fund as long as you
own it. You do it by reinvesting gains and dividends and
adding additional money. When you buy stocks, many
companies allow you to reinvest any dividends paid in
more stock at whatever the current price is. And, some
will allow you to make direct investments for fractional
shares as long as it's done through the company.

    Successful investors practice the art of DCA. Let's say
you invest $100 in your favorite fund on the 10th of
each month. Today the cost is $15 per share. Last month
it was $14.50, and the month before, $13. By averaging

the three prices, your actual cost is $14.17 per share ($15 + 14.50 + 13 = $42.50; $42.50/3 = $14.17). Not the lowest price—but never the highest either.

- *Take enough risk.* There's all kinds of risk—your age, health, taxes, inflation/deflation, emotional, even wealth. If you have health issues that may require immediate money; age issues that may require money needed for assisted type living arrangements; money owed for a large tax gain; a minimal sized nest egg; or not sure if the economy is deflating or inflating, and feel fearful that you will lose your money or be wiped out, your investments will be affected. Your risk factor is low.

  If you don't have to deal with age, health, taxes, inflation/deflation and have a comfortable nest egg, and you understand that you could lose money in an investment, you are able to take on investments that carry more risk.

- *Avoid hot tips.* They are merely that—hot and can cool off in a nano-second.

Investing is not genetic. You learn by doing—which means you will make a few mistakes along your way. The key is to learn from them, and not to repeat.

***To Do:*** Turn investing into a project. If you have kids, include them. They like the idea of making money.

- Have family members identify favorite products. Ask them to find out what company makes them and if the company sells shares of stock.
- Subscribe to a publication, such as *Money* magazine.
- Contact the National Association of Investors Corporation 856.988.6560 or *Better-Investing.org* to get information about starting an investment club.
- At a toy store, get several piles of play money— toss anything under $1,000. Or create coupons in $1,000, $5,000 and $10,000 denominations. You can also get copies of actual U.S. dollars—reduce or increase their size—there are rules. Check out your local coin shop.

  Then, give each family member a mythical $100,000. Tell them to invest their "money" in stocks that they think will increase in value. Over dinner once a month, have each investor report how his or her stocks are doing. Adults should partner with kids under 10.

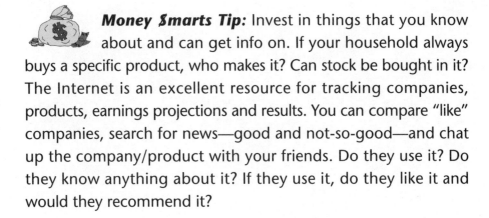***Money $marts Tip:*** Invest in things that you know about and can get info on. If your household always buys a specific product, who makes it? Can stock be bought in it? The Internet is an excellent resource for tracking companies, products, earnings projections and results. You can compare "like" companies, search for news—good and not-so-good—and chat up the company/product with your friends. Do they use it? Do they know anything about it? If they use it, do they like it and would they recommend it?

# 26   To Market, To Market

*Investing is like grocery shopping—*
*variety and bargains everywhere.*

**To Think About:** Investing can be done many ways. For the purpose of this day, I'm going to focus on the most probable place you will start: mutual funds and stocks. I know that you may invest in other areas and that there is a vast menu to choose from.

**Let's start with stocks.** You can buy shares in thousands of companies—anywhere from one share to mega thousands. When you do, you become a part owner (in most cases, very small), sharing when earnings/profits are both good and bad.

If a company is reporting a banner year, the value of the stock may increase. It can decide to pay its shareholders (you) part of the profits in the form of a dividend. The dividend can be either in cash or in more stock. Or the company could declare a stock split.

A great example is Microsoft. A $1,000 investment in Microsoft in the early 80s would be worth more that $400,000 in 2009. The shares bought in the 80s received multiple stock splits—two-for-one and three-for-twos. This means that if you had 10 shares and a two-for-one split was declared, you would now have 20 shares; if a three-for-two split had been declared, you would have 15 shares.

For growth, stocks that have a history of paying stock dividends (not cash) and/or stock splits outperform those that do not. Companies that are aggressively growing don't give cash to shareholders (at least not much). Instead, additional stock through stock dividends and splits are the preferred method to "reward" shareholders.

If the company is not doing well, its stock value can decline. If it pays a dividend, it may decide to not pay one. If this happens, it usually means that the value of its stock will also go down. Investors don't like it when companies reduce or eliminate a dividend.

Great profits are not a guarantee that stocks will increase in value. And having no profits, even reported losses, may not cause a stock to decline. Why?—investors may interpret the reported profits as "not good enough" or the reported loss as "not as bad as expected, so therefore the company is doing OK."

An excellent source for getting information is at your fingertips and possibly a short drive. The Internet is a wealth of information and accessible 24 hours a day. Your public library carries a myriad of investment references. One of them is called *The Value Line Investment Survey*. Over 1800 companies are included with updated reports released on a quarterly basis.

Stocks can be purchased through any stock broker, a discount broker and in some cases, directly from the company. The Low Cost Investment Plan of the National Association of Investors at 877-275-6242 has a special program for investors who buy only a few shares of stock at a time.

***Mutual funds pool money and buy stocks, bonds and money market instruments.*** This means that thousands, usually millions, of investors put their money into a pot—the pool—with a mutual fund company.

It then purchases the type of securities as stated within its prospectus, a booklet required by the SEC (Securities and Exchange Commission) to be given to a prospective investor. Information about the manager, objectives of the fund, what the portfolio owns at its latest reporting period, risks, etc., are included.

Most funds have a family of funds. Another menu. You can select a fund that buys communication, technology or even gold stocks. Some have dozens of different types of funds to invest in.

And, with a phone call, instructions via the Internet or by regular mail, you can switch back and forth.

> When you buy shares in a fund, you are spreading your risk. Your money is diversified into a multitude of different securities.

There are two basic types of mutual funds—load and no-load. *Load*, meaning that a commission is charged and *no-load*, meaning that no commission is charged to the investor.

Recent studies by the NASD (National Association of Securities Dealers) reported that 80% of the population didn't know what a no-load fund was! Nothing is free, even with no-load funds. An internal administrative charge is spelled out in the prospectus.

When a fund is an *open-ended* fund, it means that the number of shares it can sell is almost unlimited. A *close-ended* fund means that there are only so many shares—it trades as a common stock does.

Open-ended funds trade at NAV—net asset value. NAV is determined by taking the total value of all holdings within the fund and dividing that amount by the number of shares outstanding at the end of the trading day.

Load funds are primarily bought through stock brokers and financial planners. No-load funds are bought through the companies directly, discount brokers and some financial planners. Either can be bought via the Internet.

If you commit to an automatic monthly investment program, you can purchase a mutual fund for as low as $100 per month as an adult (sometimes less for kids). If you invest less than $100 monthly, expect that the fund will require you to sign an automatic deduction to your checking or savings account each month.

Whenever you invest, have some guidelines for what you expect to get. What profit would you like—50% increase in three years? 100%? If your investment reaches your goal within the timeframe—you have some decisions to make—sell, hold, maybe buy more.

And, set a downside price—what's your comfort level? How much will you let your investment decline before you declare it over? Set that at the time you first buy. If it hits that amount, you sell. No exceptions. Yes, I know it may come back . . . but it could take years and there are no guarantees. Take your marbles and find another opportunity.

 **To Do:**

- Attend a lecture or seminar offered by a stock broker or financial planner. Your purpose is to listen. What are

they offering? Do you understand the concept? If
you had money, would you buy it? Why? Why not?
Be aware most firms offer "free" programs to lure
in new clients. You are never obligated to become
a client.

- If you have kids, suggest that they track the value of
  Walt Disney & Co. for a few months. Have them report
  their findings at dinner. Write to the company and get
  a copy of its annual report. See if there was an increase
  in stock value when a hit movie was released (i.e. Lion
  King, Toy Story, Bolt or Wall-E).
- Buy one share of stock for each of your kids—a great
  way to get them interested in the market. Some companies offer discounts and perks to shareholders
  (Wrigley sends gum).
- Enroll in a class at the community college on investing.
- Get a copy of *The Value Line Investment Survey* on a
  company that everyone in your family is familiar with
  (your local library usually subscribes).
- Call a discount stock broker, such as Charles Schwab or
  Fidelity (or go online, *Schwab.com* or *Fidelity.com*), and
  ask for them to send you information on investing in
  the stock market. Within a few days, you will receive a
  packet of information on how to buy and sell stocks

and mutual funds. It is unlikely that you will be
pestered with follow-up phone calls.

- Visit a stock brokerage firm with your kids and ask for
any free pamphlets that explain the workings of the
stock market.

- Check out Day 30 for resources on books, websites,
and other programs available for increasing your investment knowledge.

***Money Smarts Tip:*** When you invest, don't buy and
then forget what you have. Both stocks and mutual
fund investments need to be monitored. If you hit your objectives
(an increase in value)—you need to reassess your holdings. Do
you think it will continue to increase? Stay at the same level? Not
sure? Decline?

If you think it will continue to increase—raise your price objective to a new level and continue to monitor.

If you are not sure—sell half and invest in another company and
let the balance ride, but increase your price objective. Pay your
taxes on the gain.

If you think it will stay at the same price level—why stay in it? If
it's paying a dividend, it might make sense to; if not, your money
might work better someplace else. Pay taxes on gains when you sell.

If you believe it will decline—sell now and pay your taxes on the gain. Congratulations on your savvy investment strategy.

> Profits are like the fruit on a tree. If you don't pick them when they are ripe, they fall and rot.

# 27 Investing in Yourself

*By learning new things, you reinvent yourself.*

**To Think About:** Change is everywhere. In your workplace, within your circle of friends and in your family. Best-selling book lists routinely include business and self-help offerings that charge the reader to embrace and grow through change . . . it's good for you.

One of the best ways to survive and thrive with change, is to learn something new. According to ongoing research, people who continue to learn new things, skills, even trivia, are healthier. One startling fact is that when you learn new things, you are 300% less likely to get Alzheimer's disease. That's worth reading a book and attending a class or two!

When you keep on learning, you will keep on earning. It will be rare for anyone to have the same job or work at the same function for a work lifetime. Experts project that today's employee will have anywhere from five to ten careers. This year, you may work in the healthcare administration field. In five years, your background in healthcare administration could lead you to a new career and position as an executive director of a foundation. This year, your department may be eliminated. Next year, you may be the CEO of a start-up company whose birthing ground was your basement. Change, it's everywhere.

The way you get ready for the future is by starting today. Anyone interested in being employed beyond a job that pays minimum wage must embark upon a path of continuing education. It doesn't matter if it's formal education in a university, a specific or technical school or a one day course at a local community college. The secret is to begin learning new things, new skills and new tasks.

> When you invest in yourself, you expand your education and knowledge base. You become the creator of your future.

Today's workplace demands that you know how to use a personal computer and be Internet savvy. Access to the Internet enables you to expand your information world. Websites like *Google.com, Clutsy.com,* and *Yahoo.com* are gateways to an incredible universe of knowledge—and all at your fingertips. All you need to do is activate them and get to work!

 **To Do:**

- Enroll in a computer or Internet class at your local community college.
- If you feel totally "lost," hire a kid—any child today over the age of 8 is incredibly computer savvy. It can be your child, grandchild, the kid next door—just a kid. Pay them for their time—minimum wage works and set it up that you get a "tutoring" several hours a week for a couple of weeks. Where you and I think of computers as tools, anyone under 30 views them as part of the circulatory system—they live, breathe and sleep them!
- If you don't have one, get an E-mail address.
- Create a Family website—this is a great project for the kids and grandkids to head up. Family members can post photos (this is where all those digital camera photos can land), swap silly jokes, share recipes, post a monthly or quarterly family newsletter, start planning a reunion, or just stay in touch. There are a myriad of ways to use a Family website. Imagine this—if Gramma

is in the hospital and there is a wireless connection available—family members from all over can send her get-well notes and photos. The bonus is you learn lots about technology that is at your fingertips and a must-learn.

- Have working members of your family do a self-assessment. Identify what their skills are. Are they used in their present work? Do they have skills they would like to use, but don't or can't in a current job? If there was a magic wand, would anyone change jobs? What would be the ideal job and one to work in?

- Contact your community college, college or university and find out what courses are offered in the area you are presently working in as well as in the one(s) that you would create if the magic wand was in hand.

- Find out if your employer funds or reimburses any educational costs.

- Create a project with each of your kids that teaches them (and you) something you didn't already know.

- Create a family outing and attend a scientific event at your local museum.

- Ask each person what was most interesting and what he or she learned.

- Learn to play a computer game with other family members.
- Purchase a CD encyclopedia program, such as Encarta, and randomly assign family members "let's learn about" projects. Tell them that they get to do a show-and-tell on it on a specific dinner night for the whole family. If you don't have family living with you, do it with a group of friends.

***Money $mart Tip:*** The person you are and will become will be based on the books you read, the programs you attend, the things you learn, and the people you meet. You can't afford to get behind the eight-ball when it comes to learning new things in your career and in your personal life. It's a **Money $marts** move to become Internet savvy.

# Part VII
## Building Your Resources

## (Days 28 – 30)

# 28  Don't Fall for a Bad Deal

*When in doubt, don't pay any money out.*

**To Think About:** No one likes to lose money, yet it happens every day. It's estimated that Americans lose over $300 billion annually to scams and fraud. Telemarketing fraud amounts to $60 billion alone. The most common months for a "sting" are during the summer.

The most likely targets are women and seniors. Both may be lonely and welcome the attention they get, although temporary, from a con artist. No one wants to appear stupid or foolish. Many who are conned are conned because they feared asking questions since they didn't want to look stupid or resist the pressure tactics of a persistent salesperson.

At the turn of the century, lotteries were popping up everywhere. Con-artists and crooks follow the money; they aren't dummies. One of the hottest scams was called the Canadian Lottery.

People, mostly women, were conned over the phone. It went something like this:

### Con Charlie

Hello, Mrs. Smith. I'm so glad that I got a hold of you—this is your lucky day. Are you sitting down? I'm Charlie Edwards with the Canadian Lottery Association in Montreal. Your phone number has been randomly selected this month as our runner-up winner ...

### Mrs. Smith

My, oh my—all those years I've bought those tickets ...

### Con Charlie

...I know, I buy those tickets all the time and I just keep hoping that someone will come to my door with a check . . . well, let me tell you what you've won ...

### Mrs. Smith

...Yes, tell me please—you sound like such a nice young man.

### Con Charlie

Why, why, thank you—you sound like a nice person too. Mrs. Smith, I'm so thrilled to tell you that you have won $200,000! Our first place winner got $500,000. Some months it's a little more, but I'm sure you could use that amount, couldn't you?

### Mrs. Smith

Oh, my God! My dreams have come true. How do I get my money, Charlie?

### Con Charlie

Oh, it's so simple. You just tell me you want it—I need you to fax me a copy of your driver's license. Then, you just have to pay the Canadian Export Tax on it, and the money is transferred to the bank account you tell us to wire it to, or we can send you certified funds. It's your choice.

### Mrs. Smith

Oh, young man, I can do all that—but what's an Export Tax?

## Con Charlie

I bet you could use it—heck, I could use that kind of money too. An Export Tax is what we have to tax winners who aren't citizens of Canada. For winners of $200,000, the tax is 5% or $10,000 of the amount won, which is less than what you would pay in the States. Your money is in an escrow account; when we receive the tax money, it's immediately transferred to your account or sent certified—however you would like it. Which would work best for you? . . .

Mrs. Smith sends the money to Charlie. Charlie receives it. No money is ever transferred or wired to Mrs. Smith's account. She's been conned.

And so it goes. The TV show, *60 Minutes*, did an expose on one of the "Con Charlies" who was on his way to prison. Millions of dollars had been scammed from women and men who thought they had won a real lottery.

---

Every state has a Consumer Protection Act. Use it to your benefit and for the benefit of those you care about. Both the Better Business Bureau and the State Attorney General's Office, Consumer Fraud Division, have toll free hot lines. Use them.

***To Do:*** Talk with your family members about their different experiences when they have lost money because of some type of misrepresentation or scheme. To start the discussion, share one of your experiences. Others will open up when you, wise person, parent and spouse or partner that you are, reveal a mishap from the past.

- Call your state Attorney General's office and ask what types of scams are prevalent in your area. Request a free copy of *The Real Deal: Playing the Buying Game*, an excellent resource for fraud prevention.
- Download a copy of *Schemes, Scams and Flim Flams* by going to the website, *State.sd.us/puc/2001/Publications01/ scam.pdf.* Published by the National Consumers League, it offers advice on how to avoid being taken by con artists like the individuals bilking those with the promise of winning a lottery. Share your readings with your parents and other adults in your family.
- Check out *Fraud.org* for updated schemes that are floating around, especially around the Internet. Online complaint forms are available. You can also call the National Fraud hotline at 800-876-7060 for additional information.
- Watch for stories in the news about cons and frauds and

share them with others in your family. Ask them how they would have avoided the situation.

- Most major television and radio stations in your area have consumer reporters. Call the station and ask who it is. Call that person and ask what kinds of consumer fraud are in the news.

- Next time you get a mailing that offers a prize for nothing, free vacations, sweepstakes, home improvements, or loans if you have bad credit, be suspicious. Call your local Better Business Bureau and your state Attorney General's office and ask if any complaints have been filed against the group offering the "deal." If there has, avoid it at all costs. And, anything sent by bulk mail is junk—dump it.

***Money $marts Tip:*** Whenever something sounds like it's too good to be true, it usually is 99.99999% of the time. Be suspicious and check out any deal that promises you lots. It's probably a hoax.

# **29** Hiring the Experts

*Some people are more loyal to their advisors
than they are to their own money.*

**To Think About:** Many people don't think they use financial advisors, yet they use them all the time. Consider this: if you
have bought or sold a house, you interacted with someone who
handles loans, title insurance, possibly a Realtor®; if you have a
credit card or have opened a bank account, purchased insurance
or ever bought or sold one share of stock or a mutual fund, you
have used a financial advisor.

Have you ever casually asked a friend, relative or a neighbor
about something that involved money? If you have, you enlarged
your circle of "advisors." If you have ever had someone do your
taxes or sought the opinion or advice of a lawyer on a matter
that could impact you financially, you have received financial
advice. Financial advisors are everywhere; some good, some not-
so-good.

Just about anyone can call himself or herself a financial planner today. Even you. No special licenses or regulation. Just hang a sign out, and you're in business! A few years ago, *Consumer Reports* surveyed forty banks that sold mutual funds to customers. Seventy-five percent of the bank salespeople gave out inaccurate and wrong information!

> You get advice from experts because you don't have time, knowledge and/or desire to do it on your own. In some areas, such as investing, you need someone to process a purchase or sale, even when no advice is given!

 ***To Do:*** It's time to take inventory. Who are the men and women in your life that affect you financially?

- Make a complete list of all the individuals who you presently work with. Include phone numbers, addresses, company affiliations and what they do for you. If any policies or contracts are in force, attach their numbers for tracking and a copy of the front page.
- If you are unhappy with any of your advisors, take steps to replace them. Now. Begin by asking friends and colleagues for referrals. Don't forget to ask about

advisors who have not worked out and why. In financial planning, two sources to go to are the Financial Planning Association (*FPANET.org*) and the National Association of Personal Financial Advisors (*NAPFA.org*). If a divorce is a possibility, the Financial Divorce Association offers a variety of services and publications (*FDADivorce.com*).

- Set up a criteria to ask of your potential advisors. Include questions regarding areas of expertise, credentials and training, years spent in the area (five years should be a minimum), how they get paid (commissions, fees—hourly or flat— or a combination . . . *nothing* is free), and references (ask for individuals whom they have advised for a minimum of three years and have similar objectives as yours).

- If the advisor/planner sells financial products, what's the commission? You have every right to know how much he is getting paid. Will he get any other type of financial benefits/perks from the other professionals that you are referred to?

- Ask what mistakes or wrong advice they have made in the past (if they say none—walk away . . . everyone makes mistakes). Always ask what is their preference for working with clients—they call you, you call them only (know what yours is before asking this question).

- If the advisor is someone who will be making recommendations for investing your money—ask how their personal portfolios are doing. If they won't reveal or show you how they have done with their own investments—I'd take a pass. You want someone who is successful in their own financial planning and investment options—if they can't do a decent job on their own, what do you think they are going to do with your money?

- Most planners put things in writing—a client agreement or engagement letter—ask if the ones you are interviewing do. And, if they don't, why don't they?

- Make a calendar note for the next year to make an appointment with the advisor(s) you've selected to review your financial status and direction.

---

Trust your gut instincts. If you feel queasy and unsure when interviewing an expert, leave. Do not work with anyone who pushes you to buy. Ever.

**Money $marts Tip:** When seeking financial advice, don't hold back—it's time for full disclosure: what you have to work with, what your concerns are and what your goals are. **Money $marts** begins with believing in yourself, in understanding that you have a unique ability to turn possibilities into realities. It begins with your own intuitive insights.

# 30

## Your Money $marts Resource Center

*Get all the advice you can and be wise the rest of your life.*
*Proverbs 19: 20*

***To Think About:*** Few people are "naturally" blessed with **Money $marts**. They learn about it the old fashioned way—by reaching out, reading, playing games . . . and by making mistakes. All lead to learning. You learn about money, especially with investing your money, two ways.

First, when your investment increases in value—always a goal in the investment arena—and your strategies work well, you learn from it. Let's look at the flip side. What happens when you lose money? Guess what, most likely, you learn again! I know, this isn't the fun way, but it happens.

To help reduce your learning curve, I've assembled a library of information. Yes, we know that many of the books, magazines and games are available in a favorite spot, the public library. But, here's one of the money secrets I've learned over the years: develop your own "library." Willingly write in your books—use high-light and Post-it® notes. With pencil (or pen), high-lighter and pad of Post-its, you'll have millions of dollars of advice at your fingertips.

*To Do:* Begin to assemble your personal **Money $marts Library**—for the adults and kids in your family. Contact used book stores as well as new. Play Monopoly with the family (also Junior Monopoly for younger kids)—this is the granddaddy of money games.

## Internet Sites—

The Internet is rich with information. Where books can be referred back to, easily accessed and loaded with charts and graphs that you can take pencil and pen to, the Internet can deliver information to your fingertips within seconds. With websites like *Google.com* and *Yahoo.com*, just type in a word or two and you are linked to an unbelievable number of information sites. Sites like *Fool.com, Money.com, Schwab.com, Fidelity.com* and *Vanguard.com* all contain a stream of current information available to customers and non-customers alike.

Below are just a few of the many, many money-oriented websites. A good website changes its content often—some throughout the day. Probe the ones below and make it a habit to check back with your favorites to see the latest in news and strategies that tie in with your personal money goals.

Depending on the search engine you use, you may have to add "<u>www.</u>" in front of each, then the rest of the website address below. The websites below have been referenced throughout **Money $marts.**

## Advisory
*AICPA.org* (accounting and tax)
*CPAPFS.org* (accounting and tax)
*FDADivorce.com* (divorce information/consulting)
*FPANET.org* (financial planning)
*NAEA.org* (accounting and tax)
*NAPFA.org* (financial advisors)

## College
*CollegeAnswer.com* (Sallie Mae loans)
*CollegeBoard.com* (financial aid and loans)
*CollegeSavings.com* (college savings and CDs)
*FAFSA.ed.gov* (federal student aid)
*FastWeb.com* (financial aid and loans)
*SRNExpress.com* (scholarship search)

## Credit

*AnnualCreditReport.com* (credit reports)

*BankRate.com* (credit card rates)

*CardRatings.com* (compare credit cards)

*CardWeb.com* (compare credit cards)

*CCCSintl.org* (consumer credit counseling)

*ConsumersUnion.org* (dispute credit information)

*CreditCards.com* (compare credit cards)

*Equifax.com* (credit reporting – Equifax)

*Experian.com* (credit reporting – Experian)

*FTC.gov/credit* (dispute credit information)

*GulfStreamFinancialCorp.com; SharipDebtFree.com* (get debt free)

*Mapping-your-future.org/paying/cnsldte* (fed. loan consolidation)

*MyFICO.com* (credit scoring)

*OptOutPrescreen.com* (block credit offers)

*TUC.com* (credit reporting - TransUnion)

## General

*AARP.org* (the spot for anyone over 50 to browse)

*CharityNavigator.com* (rates over 5,000 charities)

*Google.com* (Google site for general information)

*Yahoo.com* (Yahoo! site for general information)

*SSA.gov* (Social Security)

*Quicken.com* (Quicken financial software updates)

## Health Care
*AssurantHealth.com* (short term health policies)
*Choices.org* (health care durable power of attorney)
*eHealthInsurance.com* (short term health policies)

## Insurance
*InsuranceQuote.com* (low cost insurance)
*SelectQuote.com* (low cost insurance)
*TermQuote.com* (low cost insurance)
*WeissRatings.com* (financial safety ratings)

## Investments
*Finance.com* (Yahoo's financial articles)
*Fool.com* (Motley Fool)
*CNBC.com* (CNBC news/TV)
*CNN.com* (CNN and Money magazine)
*CBSMarketWatch.com* (financial news – CBS)
*Fidelity.com* (Fidelity mutual funds)
*Kiplinger.com* (online calculators)
*InvestorGuide.com* (over 1,000 FAQs)
*Morningstar.com* (mutual fund ratings)
*Schwab.com* (Charles Schwab & Co.)
*Vanguard.com* (Vanguard mutual funds)

## Legal Issues

*LegacyWriter.com* (wills and trust software)
*MakeYourWill.com* (wills software)
*Nolo.com* (info on all things legal)
*StandardLegal.net* (legal info and software)

## Associations for You—

There are more groups and associations that you can connect with when it comes to money advice. Here's a few that are worthwhile to know about:

* *Financial Planning Association*—call 800-282-PLAN (7526) or go to website *FPANET*.org. It offers a freebie— *How a Financial Planner Can Help You and How to Choose the Right One*. FPA is an association whose members are financial planners or affiliated with financial planning.

  Here's some of the alphabet soup you'll find within the group—Certified Financial Planners (CFP), Chartered Financial Analysts (CFA), Chartered Mutual Fund Consultant (CMFC), Certified Fund Specialist (CFS), Enrolled Agents (EA), Certified Public Accountants (CPA), Personal Financial Specialist (PFS), lawyer (JD) and Financial Divorce Analyst (FDA). There are others out there, but these professions will be the majority of members.

- *National Association of Personal Financial Advisors*—call 888-FEE-ONLY (333-6659) to connect with fee-only financial advisors. Their freebie is called *Why Select a Fee-Only Financial Advisor.* Website is *NAPFA.org.*
- *American Institute of Certified Public Accountants*—call 888-777-7077 to request a CPA who is also a PFS (Personal Financial Specialist). You can also go to the website, *CPAPFS.org* for information.
- *Financial Divorce Association*—call 888-332-3342 to request a referral of a Certified Financial Planner™ Professional, Lawyer or Certified Public Accountant who specializes in divorce. The website is *FDADivorce.com.*
- *American Institute of Certified Public Accountants*—call 212-596-6200 or go to the Website, *AICPA.org.* If you don't have any accounting professional referrals, your state CPA association will assist you.
- *National Association of Enrolled Agents*—call 800-424-4339 or go the Website, *NAEA.org.* Enrolled agents can represent you before the IRS, as a CPA can as well.
- *American Association of Individual Investors* provides investment education in retirement, investing basics,

and financial planning. It's a nonprofit whose goal is to provide tools so that you are more effective. Its website is *AAII.com* and phone # 800-428-2244.

- *National Association of Investors Corporation* is the key contact for anyone who is interested in creating an investment club. Supplies all the forms, tax reporting info and a monthly publication for each member of a club, *Better Investing.* Call 877-275-6242 for information or go to the website, *Better-Investing.org.*

**Books for You—**
*Directory of Companies Offering Dividend Reinvestment Plans.* Evergreen Enterprises, 2002. Recommend getting this at your local library.

**Briles, Judith** *The Confidence Factor.* Denver: Mile High Press, 2008.
_____ , **and Wilson, Carol Ann** *The Dollars and Sense of Divorce.* Chicago: Dearborn Publishing, 1998.
**Chatzky, Jean** *Pay It Down! From Debt to Wealth on $10 a Day.* New York: Portfolio, 2004.
_____ *You Don't Have to Be Rich: Comfort, Happiness, and Financial Security on Your Own Terms.* New York: Portfolio, 2003.
_____ *Talking Money.* New York: Warner Business Books, 2002.
**Johnson, Dennis** *Do This.* Denver: Minor Street Publishing, 2007.

**Orman, Suze** *Women and Money-Owning the Power to Control Your Destiny.* New York: Spiegel & Grace, 2007.

_____ *The Money Book for the Young, Fabulous and Broke.* New York: Riverhead, 2007.

**Quinn, Jane Bryant** *Making the Most of Your Money Now-The Classic Bestseller Completely Revised for the New Economy.* New York: Simon & Schuster, 2009.

_____ *Smart and Simple Financial Strategies for Busy People.* New York: Simon & Schuster, 2006.

**Schwab, Charles** *You're Fifty—Now What? Investing for the Second Half of Your Life.* New York: Three Rivers Press, 2002.

_____ *Charles Schwab's New Guide to Financial Independence Completely Revised and Updated: Practical Solutions for Busy People.* New York: Three Rivers Press, 2004.

**Tobias, Andrew** *The Only Other Investment Guide You'll Ever Need.* New York: Harvest Books, 2004.

**Tyson, Eric** *Investing for Dummies, 5th Edition.* New York: John Wiley & Sons, Inc., 2008.

_____ *Mutual Funds for Dummies, 5th Edition.* New York: John Wiley & Sons, Inc., 2007.

_____ *Personal Finance for Dummies, 5th Edition.* New York: John Wiley & Sons, Inc., 2006.

**Wilson, Carol Ann** *The Survival Manual for Men in Divorce.* Boulder: Omni Press, 2004.

_____ The Survival Manual for Women in Divorce. Boulder: Omni Press, 2004.

_____ and **Wall, Ginita** *ABCs of Divorce for Women.* Boulder: Quantum Press, 2003.


**Books for Kids—**
**Bochner, Authur, Bochner, Rose and Berg, Adrian** *The New Totally Awesome Money Book for Kids.* New York: Newmarket, 2007.

_____ *Totally Awesome Business Book for Kids.* New York: Newmarket, 2007.

**Briles, Judith** *Money $marts for Kids.* Denver: Mile High Press, 2009.

**Gardner, David** *The Motley Fool Investment Guide for Teens.* New York: Fireside, 2002.

**Harman, Hollis Page** *Money Sense for Kids.* New York: Barrons Education Series, 2005.

**Karlitz, Gail** *Growing Money: A Complete Investing Guide for Kids,* New York: Price Stern Sloan, 2001.

**Sember, Brette McWhorten** *The Everything Kids Money Book: From Savings, to Spending, to Investing.* New York: Adams Media, 2008.

**Parker Brothers**, *Monopoly.*

## Periodicals and Magazines—

*Money*
800-633-9970
*Money.com*

*The New York Times*
866-228-8717
*NYTimes.com/sb-subscription*

*Kiplinger's Personal Finance*
888-419-0424
*Kiplinger.com*

*Smart Money*
800-444-4204
*SmartMoney.com*

*Value Line Investment Survey*
212-907-1500
*ValueLine.com*

*The Wall Street Journal*
800-568-7625
*WSJ.com*

*The Individual's Guide to
No-Load Mutual Funds*
800-428-2244
*AAII.com*

*Schemes, Scams and Flim Flams* identifies what kind of cons to look for. You can download it at *State.sd.us/puc/2001/Publications01/scam.pdf.*

The Low Cost Investment Plan of the National Association of Investors at 877-275-6242 or *Better-Investing.org/about/lowcost* has a special program for investors who buy only a few shares of stock at a time.

## Tax and Bookkeeping Software

The prices listed below were current when this book went to print. As with everything, there are bound to be changes. You may find rebates and discounts on any of them. No matter, I think they are a bargain and the use of a money software program is a must. Here's a few that work well:

| | |
|---|---|
| Turbo Tax | $52.99 |
| MacInTax | $38.99 |
| Quicken | $49.95 |
| MicroSoft Money | $49.95 |
| Quickbooks | $159.99 |

***Money $marts Tip:*** If you have kids, money games like Monopoly and the Reward Game are excellent sources to learn from. Games that include counting and numbers, such as Rummikub (advanced), and Gin Rummy and Crazy Eights (beginners) are always good to just get kids thinking.

Congratulations! You've completed the first month—30 days that are guaranteed to change your financial life.

# Month 2

# Adding It All Up!

*Work brings profit; talk brings poverty.*
*Proverbs 14:23*

There are few overnight successes. Getting your money act together within a 30-day period is an exception—it's equivalent to an overnight success! Many of the activities recommended during the first 30 days can't be measured until more time has gone by. Schedule your calendar to review your *Spending Plan* at the end of every month throughout this first year. By then, it will be a habit . . . which is a very good thing.

Let's review what you've done in the past 30 days . . . it's been a HUGE undertaking—

- ✔ You've learned about having and using money and how to get organized.
- ✔ You've examined why appropriate insurance needs to be in place and regularly reviewed.

✔ You've addressed the need to save and invest, to *tithe* to yourself.

✔ You've considered some of the ways to begin an investment program.

✔ You've explored why and how the misuse and overuse of credit can harm your financial security.

✔ You've identified characteristics of competent money advisors.

✔ You've looked at kids and money and why you should teach them about its purpose.

✔ You've discussed the need to start planning to retire today.

✔ You've created forms, activities and action items for you and your family to use and do.

A few other thoughts that need your follow-through:

• If you found errors in your credit report or it includes negative information from your past, only time will clear them up. Erroneous items will eventually be removed— with your persistence. Negative, but accurate, reports can only be softened by changing your ways.

Do not pay one penny to anyone or a group that promises to "clean up" your credit rating. It's done by eliminating late payments, reducing and getting rid of balances, collections and the like. Creditors want to see a minimum "clean record" for two years.

If the misuse or overuse of credit has been a problem, vow that nothing new comes into your house unless it is absolutely vital to the family.

- Every time you make a mortgage or rent payment, another check should be directed toward your savings account and/or investment account—your tithe to your future financial independence.

  Here are two other ways to support an automatic tithe. Direct your payroll department to automatically deposit a specific amount to a savings or credit union account; or, sign up for an automatic monthly withdrawal program with a mutual fund company or brokerage firm from your checking or savings account. Money can be directed to a variety of funds, including a money market account and stocks.

- You and your family's sleuthing have probably revealed several areas that money has been frittered away. Fast food meals, too many meals eaten out, money spent for overpriced convenience foods, impulse buying, and no real Spending Plan in place will most likely head the list. Most likely, you will save thousands of dollars a year

when you step away from choosing the convenience
route and impulse buying—THOUSANDS of DOLLARS!

The fact that you have worked through this book deserves a
standing ovation from me. I salute your persistence and commitment and encourage you to continue your **Money $marts** jour-
ney. With each new twist and turn in your daily life, you will find
that the past 30 days will lay the foundation for financial security
for the rest of your life. It's been a challenging month—but one
that you won't regret. A huge Bravo to you!

> Your money mantra should become: If it doesn't fit into my
> Spending Plan, it isn't bought. Period.

*Money $marts Tip:* Being **Money $mart** means that
you will drop the old ways that weren't working for you
and develop and embrace new habits for the rest of your life.
Here's my Top 10:

**1. Know where kiss-off dollars have gone.**
   Ninety-nine percent of us—smart and not so smart—have

dribbled away money. Your new motto is "No More Lost Bucks."

2. **Set up a savings and investment plan early on**.
   You may have started one, or both, but didn't really grasp the concept or simple formula that— savings + investing = money security for life.

3. **Be consistent and committed from the beginning.**
   It's easy for youthfulness and naiveté to get in the way. After all, tomorrow was another day. Now tomorrow, lots of them, have come and gone. They're yesterdays. Just work on today—what do you need to do today?

4. **Spread your money into several possibilities.**
   Savings is savings and investing is . . . well, it does keep changing, but there are the basics. Opportunities are everywhere. **Money $mart** investors learn that you don't put all your eggs in one basket. Diversifying is critical for money growth and security.

5. **Be curious, be alert, be open to new ideas and keep learning**.
   Times change, things change, you change. Don't get stuck on how things used to be. What they will be is a factor of what you choose to put into it.

6. **Talk about money with your friends, your spouse, your kids and your family**.

   The closet that holds the money secrets is not going to reside in your home. Talking relieves and removes many of the money fears you may face.

7. **Forgive yourself when you make mistakes.**

   Forgiveness is always easier to say than do. Some of the things that you do with your money won't work. It happens.

8. **Be smart when using credit.**

   You need credit and will continue to. If you don't abuse it, the credit merchants can't abuse you. A real win-win.

9. **Tithe to yourself faithfully.**

   Every time you get a paycheck, a bonus, a money gift, an investment gain, an interest or dividend payment, even "found" money, any money—salt at least 10% of it away—right off the top!

10. **Trust yourself.**

    You are as intelligent, trustworthy and competent as any financial advisor you will come across. They've just had a few more years of training and experience than you have.

## Afterword . . .

# Just Do It!

Most adults today grew up with the ditty, "One for the money, two for the show, three to get ready, and four to go." Unfortunately, when it comes to money, too many stop at step three. They spend years getting ready and more ready. They rarely go.

Having **Money $marts** means completing the last step. The actions that you take by *just doing it* will make the difference between money security and money insecurity. Doing it means that you have (or are in the process of) tracking where your money goes, you have your cash flow in control, you have the right type and amount of insurance, you have created a will and/or trust, you have identified investment opportunities and implemented a strategy of investing for the long term and have identified which money professionals you want, or need, to work with.

What do you make today? Do you spend everything, every penny of your income? What amounts of your spending are directly related to areas that *will not* be in your spending plans at retirement? Part of your planning must project out to when you want to pull back, or out, of the work-for-pay scene.

Figure that you can at least make an average of 5% to 7% return on your TOTAL savings and investments. Add that amount to the projection from what Social Security says you will receive (reduce the amount estimated by 10% if you are over 50; 20% if under—just in case there is a reduction—plus any other pensions or annuities you own or will be paid. Next, look at what you spend money on. Will. . . .

- *The kids be gone and self-sufficient when you retire?*
  (Let's hope so. Kids cost big bucks; do you know how much you really spend on them?)

- *Your home be paid off?*
  (A definite goal, how would you like to just pay real estate taxes and maintenance requirements—how much does having no mortgage payment reduce your outgo? Or, is your home too big now, and you want

something smaller, which usually costs less to purchase?
If you bought a smaller home for less dollars, you might
end up with a chunk of cash to stash.)

- *You have less to no costs for further education?* (No more
  college costs or expanding training costs related to your
  work.)
- *You be driving less?* (You may need only one car if a
  couple; your insurance coverage could be less and/or
  reduced in costs; general automotive costs may decline.)
- *You be spending less in clothing?* (Most likely yes, since
  you don't need a work wardrobe—have you ever really
  kept track of how much of your monthly expenses are
  related to appearance factors?)
- *You be spending less for convenience foods and going out
  to eat?* Many report that they actually enjoy cooking the
  old-fashioned way after they cut their work hours back
  outside of the home.
- *You be spending less on life insurance?* Insurance is
  purchased to protect dependents. If the dependents are
  on their own, your insurance costs should drop.
  Disability will not be in play if you aren't working for
  pay. It also applies to your other insurance. It is normal
  for your casualty insurance to decline—homeowners
  and automotive, when you pass 65.

- *Your federal and state tax obligations decline?* (If you are not working for pay, as you were when employed, your taxable income should be reduced.)

The answers to the above queries will most likely be yes to the above, or your goal is to have them yes. Then you need to ask, what areas will I be spending money on? Trips, learning things vocationally, grandkids (trust me, money flows in this direction), etc.—what, where and when?

When you delete the categories and amounts that will not be spent, you can realistically get to an amount that will be your estimated expense requirements years down the road. *It's this amount you need to offset against your future income.* Your retirement income will be made up of any pensions, annuities, IRAs, 401(k), 403(b), investments, savings, *and* Social Security. Social Security is not going to die, it may be adjusted a tad, but not in a draconian format that so many doomsayers seem to rejoice in shouting.

Do you need a million dollars in savings and investments when you retire? Most likely, NO. Don't let the media and financial advisors spook you.

If you have had a financial planner create a plan for you, be wary of planners who tell you that you need a minimum of a *million dollars* in your nest egg before you can have any peace of mind. This number, the mythical million bucks, needs to be held in a high degree of suspicion.

If your kids are gone, most debt is gone, your home is paid for, and insurance costs are reduced, what will be your monthly financial outgo? As much as it is today? I would say, definitely no. Unless you are planning on extensive traveling and replacing the money you no longer spend on kids, insurance, mortgage, etc. with new expenses, your monthly expenses will be reduced dramatically. Most likely, to the tune of a few thousand dollars each month.

Many of the financial projections by financial planning and investment institutions low-ball any reductions. The average household spends 30% of its money on housing and cars. When my husband and I crunched our numbers, we found that our expenses would be reduced by 60%! A far cry from the estimated 15% to 20% that was being used by some of the formula retirement projections.

The money difference between this new projected outgo and projected income is what you now focus on. Ask—

What do I need to make up the difference (if there is one)? How much more do I need to make, save and invest to supplement what it looks like I will have from my pensions, annuities, IRAs, 401(k)s, 403(b)s, investments, savings, *and* Social Security?

It's that difference between your expected income from retirement income and expected expenses you are looking to create. Being very conservative, you should be able to get a minimum of 5% to 7% on all of your investments. Let's say you find that you will experience a shortfall of $1,500 each month based on what you presently have in line for retirement income. Your question now is, "How much *more* do I need to salt away to create that $1,500 per month if I can average a 7% return on it—the principal amount?"

Let's also say that you have about 20 years until you want to retire. For an asset to generate $1,500 a month income, or 7% annually, it would have to be valued at approximately $257,000. What would you have to save or invest each year to get to your goal of $257,000? The answer is $12,850 ($257,000 / 20 = $12,850). To achieve your goal of $12,850 per year, you would need to put aside $1,071 per month ($12,850 / 12 = $1,071). Also keep in mind that number does not include any appreciation (nor inflation factors) on the $12,850, which will get you there a lot faster.

If you thought your growth and earnings would average 10% instead of 7%, you would need to set aside $8,000 per year ($667 per month); and if your average growth rate was 12 1/2%, your nut would be $6,340 per year ($533 per month). The greater the return, the lower the amount you have to put aside and/or the less time you have to save and invest.

But, always keep this in mind—the greater the return possibility, the higher the degree of risk. Be realistic in your expectations.

Over time, you will probably average anywhere from 7% to 10%—the stock market has. But it's not 10% every year; some years are more, some are less.

The key to money success is to get started. You don't have to be in the middle of the chaos that 2008 created for millions globally . . . your turbulent times could be from a costly illness, accident, job loss or some other financial misfortune. Turbulent times happen. With **Money $marts for Turbulent Times,** you will be able to get back on track.

---

When you reach your money goal on an investment, take it. Gains are like fruit on a tree . . . if you don't pick when ripe, they rot. Leave something on the table to the next person-pigs never fly.

---

No longer are you stuck with the cloud of *one for the money; two for the show; three to get ready; three to get ready, three to get ready . . . You are now in "go."*

## About the Author

# Judith Briles

**Dr. Judith Briles** is the founder of The Briles Group, Inc., a Colorado-based research, training and consulting firm. She is internationally acclaimed as a speaker and recognized as an expert in solutions to workplace and women's issues. Prior to the formation of The Briles Group, Inc. in 1987, Judith was a stockbroker and Certified Financial Planner® for 15 years.

Dr. Briles is an award-winning author of over 25 books, including: *Stabotage! How to Deal with the Pit Bulls, Skunks, Snakes, Scorpions & Slugs in the Health Care Workplace, Zapping Conflict in the Health Care Workplace, The Confidence Factor: Cosmic Gooses Lay Golden Eggs, Woman to Woman 2000, The SeXX Factor, Stop Stabbing Yourself in the Back, When God Says NO, 10 Smart Money Moves for Women,* and *Smart Money Moves for Kids.*

Judith Briles is a frequent guest on national television and radio and has appeared on over 1000 programs, including *CNN, CNNfn, Oprah, John Gray* and *Good Morning America.* Her work has been featured in numerous national and regional publications including *The Wall Street Journal, Time, Newsweek, USA Today* and *People* magazine. She writes the "Career Moves" column for the *Denver Business Journal.*

She is currently President of the Colorado Authors League (ColoradoAuthors.org) and is a Past President and/or Director of the Colorado Independent Publishers Association (CIPABooks.com), the National Speaker's Association, Gilda's Club-Denver, The WISH List, the Women's Banks and the Colorado Women's Leadership Coalition.

Colorado Biz magazine has named her company as a Top 100 in the state of Colorado. Her work has sold in excess of one million copies and has been translated into 14 languages. Judith has earned both Masters and Doctorate of Business Administration degrees. In 2004, she was named a Woman of Distinction by the Girl Scouts of America.

For information on Dr. Judith Briles' availability for speeches and workshops, to sign up for *JB's Movie Reviews* or to obtain her online newsletter, please contact her at:

**The Briles Group, Inc.**
**PO Box 460880**
**Aurora CO 80046**
**800-594-0800 ~ 303-627-9184 Fax**
**DrJudithBriles@aol.com**
*Briles.com*

# Acknowledgments

There's nothing an author likes better than to have her readers suggest book ideas. This book was seeded from *10 Smart Money Moves for Women*—men said, "Just write a book that is genderless with content," and women said, "Can you create something that gives me a To Do List to get me on track within a fairly short period of time."

I listened, heard and did what was asked. **Money $marts** is your book, it's got everything in it that can truly start the engines and keep you on track. Most of us are on a time crunch—gone are the days of the 500-plus page 'how-to" money tome.

With the advent of the multiple money disasters that the first decade of the 21st century delivered, now, more than ever, you need money smarts—lots of them.

Getting the final product to the reader always is a team effort. *Barbara Munson* quickly cut and slashed where needed and became my master editor and the perfect person to ask, "Does this make sense?"

*Shannon Parish* became my second set of eyes and co-brainstormer, always ready to offer feedback when I needed it and add her illustrating expertise in all the right areas.

*Ronnie Moore* has brilliantly formatted six of my books—she again caught my vision.

*Rebecca Finkel* is the Cover Queen. She always creates the magic that makes me smile and know it's perfect.

*Dolores Ruybal, Karen Zuppa* and *John Maling* made sure that I had the time to write.

I thank them all.      JB